SUPERMAN™

THE ULTIMATE GUIDE TO THE
MAN OF STEEL

TOUCHING MOMENT
As Krypton shattered all around them, Jor-El shared his undying love for Lara, gently caressing her cheek. It was the first and last time they would touch as their world came to a cataclysmic end.

THE KENTS

MARTHA AND JONATHAN KENT couldn't believe their eyes when the Kryptonian birthing matrix fell out of the Midwestern sky. Swerving in their old Ford pickup to avoid the impact crater, the Kents were both fascinated and afraid of the mysterious spacecraft. But their fears dissolved away when the matrix revealed its tiny infant occupant. After the childless farmers decided to raise the baby boy in their close-knit and loving home, the Kents soon learned just how unique their son would grow to be!

STAR-CHILD

Unable to have children of their own, the Kents were overjoyed to discover that a baby had seemingly been delivered to them from the stars. Jonathan Kent speculated that the infant must have traveled long and far to reach Earth. Martha Kent, meanwhile, merely saw an orphan in desperate need of a family.

FAMILY HISTORY

From letters and journals unearthed near his home, Jonathan Kent learned startling secrets about his ancestors. In 1854, abolitionist Silas Kent journeyed to Lawrence, Kansas, with his two eldest sons, Nathaniel and Jebediah, and established the town's first newspaper. However Silas Kent's anti-slavery stance led to his murder and divided his sons. During the Civil War, the good-hearted Nate sided with the Union, while trouble-prone Jeb fought alongside the Confederacy.

If separated from their super-son in an emergency, the Kents signal that they are safe by passing along a secret code-phrase: "Beef bourguignon with ketchup."

REAL NAME
Martha Clark Kent

OCCUPATION Homemaker

BASE Rural Kansas

HEIGHT 5 ft 4 in **WEIGHT** 140 lb

EYES Blue **HAIR** White

FIRST APPEARANCE
SUPERMAN #1
(Summer 1939)

AT HOME WITH THE KENTS

Besides tending their modest farm, Jonathan and Martha Kent enjoy reading and writing, and have a love of journalism passed down from their ancestor Silas Kent and perpetuated by their reporter son Clark. Jonathan is an amateur historian who continues to piece together the generational saga of the Kents. Martha maintains secret scrapbooks that chronicle the exploits of Superman.

I SAVED YOU A PIECE OF PIE...

MOTHERLY ADVICE

When her son struggles with the weight of the world upon his shoulders, Martha Kent proffers solutions full of good old-fashioned common sense and kindness.

HOME ON THE RANGE

Through blanketing blizzards and dust-bowl droughts, the Kents persevere, continuing to farm the parcel of land Nathaniel Kent settled for his family in 1871. The Kent homestead has weathered torrential rains, cyclones, and even a hover-tank attack by the super-villain Conduit! No matter what the hardship, Jonathan and Martha Kent rebuild and replant, refusing to give up the Kansas soil that their ancestors fought and died for.

AN IDYLLIC CHILDHOOD

Life on a farm isn't always a picnic, but Clark never lacked love and affection. As a toddler, he rarely appreciated his strained peas, but he grew tall and strong thanks to Martha's home cooking. He also managed to share some table scraps with the family dogs, retriever Rusty and border collie Shelby.

The Kent farm felt the fallout of Imperiex's first strike upon Earth, an assault that almost completely obliterated Topeka, Kansas.

FAMILY REUNION

Following the destruction of his farm in the Imperiex War, a wounded Jonathan Kent wandered Kansas with no memory of his past or identity. Seeing Superman on a television newscast lifted the fog of amnesia and Jonathan soon returned home to his much relieved spouse and son.

REAL NAME
Jonathan Joseph Kent

OCCUPATION Farmer

BASE Rural Kansas

HEIGHT 5 ft 8 in **WEIGHT** 175 lb

EYES Blue **HAIR** White, balding

FIRST APPEARANCE
SUPERMAN #1
(Summer 1939)

SMALLVILLE

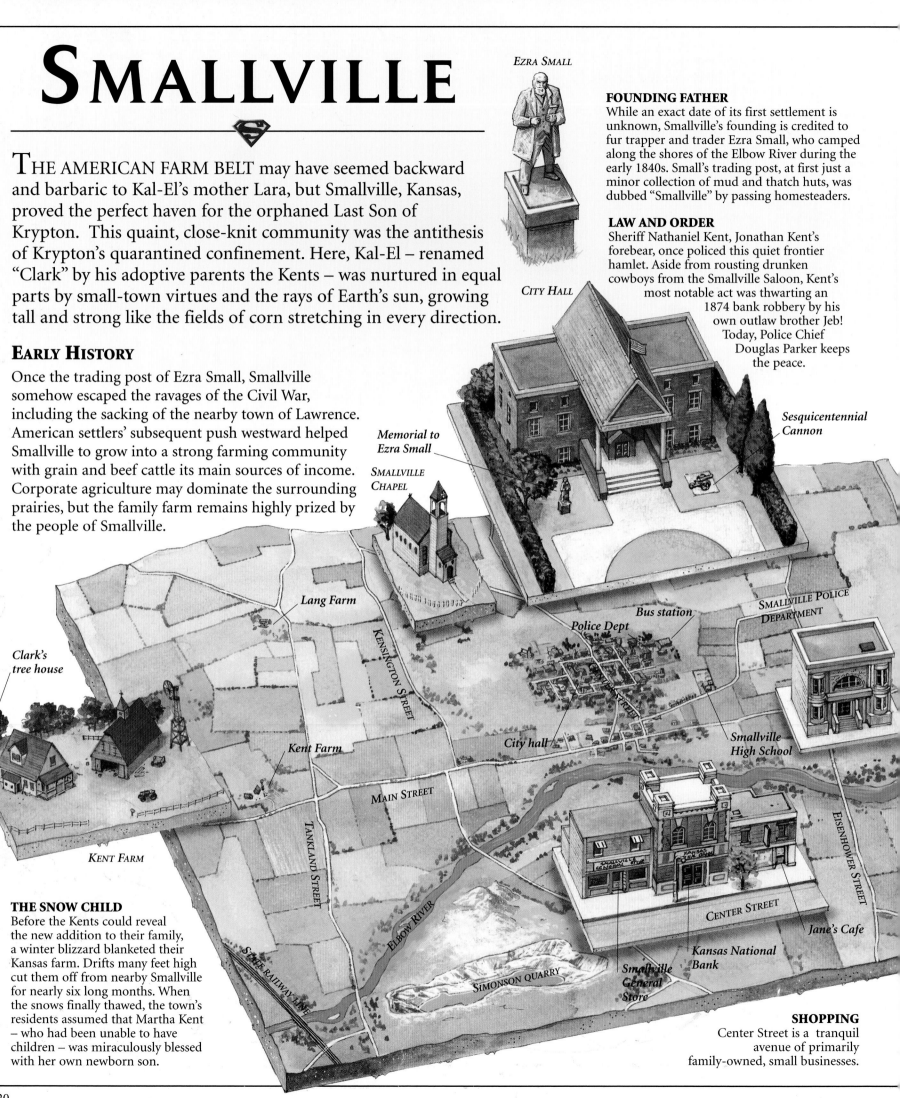

EZRA SMALL

THE AMERICAN FARM BELT may have seemed backward and barbaric to Kal-El's mother Lara, but Smallville, Kansas, proved the perfect haven for the orphaned Last Son of Krypton. This quaint, close-knit community was the antithesis of Krypton's quarantined confinement. Here, Kal-El – renamed "Clark" by his adoptive parents the Kents – was nurtured in equal parts by small-town virtues and the rays of Earth's sun, growing tall and strong like the fields of corn stretching in every direction.

EARLY HISTORY

Once the trading post of Ezra Small, Smallville somehow escaped the ravages of the Civil War, including the sacking of the nearby town of Lawrence. American settlers' subsequent push westward helped Smallville to grow into a strong farming community with grain and beef cattle its main sources of income. Corporate agriculture may dominate the surrounding prairies, but the family farm remains highly prized by the people of Smallville.

FOUNDING FATHER

While an exact date of its first settlement is unknown, Smallville's founding is credited to fur trapper and trader Ezra Small, who camped along the shores of the Elbow River during the early 1840s. Small's trading post, at first just a minor collection of mud and thatch huts, was dubbed "Smallville" by passing homesteaders.

LAW AND ORDER

Sheriff Nathaniel Kent, Jonathan Kent's forebear, once policed this quiet frontier hamlet. Aside from rousting drunken cowboys from the Smallville Saloon, Kent's most notable act was thwarting an 1874 bank robbery by his own outlaw brother Jeb! Today, Police Chief Douglas Parker keeps the peace.

CITY HALL

Memorial to Ezra Small

SMALLVILLE CHAPEL

Sesquicentennial Cannon

Lang Farm

Bus station

Police Dept

SMALLVILLE POLICE DEPARTMENT

KENSINGTON STREET

Clark's tree house

Kent Farm

City hall

Smallville High School

MAIN STREET

TANKLAND STREET

ELBOW RIVER

CENTER STREET

EISENHOWER STREET

KENT FARM

Jane's Cafe

STATE RAILWAY LINE

SIMONSON QUARRY

Smallville General Store

Kansas National Bank

THE SNOW CHILD

Before the Kents could reveal the new addition to their family, a winter blizzard blanketed their Kansas farm. Drifts many feet high cut them off from nearby Smallville for nearly six long months. When the snows finally thawed, the town's residents assumed that Martha Kent – who had been unable to have children – was miraculously blessed with her own newborn son.

SHOPPING

Center Street is a tranquil avenue of primarily family-owned, small businesses.

SMALLVILLE HIGH

A few years before the world reaped the benefits of Superman's solar-saturated Kryptonian cells, Clark's *alma mater* unknowingly witnessed the beginnings of his superpowers. While his incredible strength and speed had yet to fully emerge, Clark nevertheless developed into a star athlete, faster and more agile than his teammates on the Smallville High football team.

After scoring ten touchdowns in the season-ending championship, Clark cut short his sporting career when he learned the secret of his origins.

HE CAN FLY!
Clark realized he could fly when his dog Rusty sent him tumbling over a ravine. He had already astounded his parents by spying items through walls and hefting enormous weights. Realizing that the simple folk of Smallville might fear their son, the Kents encouraged Clark to conceal his great gifts.

...SMALLVILLE **NEVER** CHANGES

Smallville and surrounding Kansas lie in "Tornado Alley," a cyclone-prone swath of territory stretching from Texas to Minnesota. Years ago, one terrible twister tore through Main Street!

NO PLACE LIKE HOME
Clark Kent often returns to his picturesque hometown when the woes of the world abate and allow him a moment to rest and reflect. Clark values the honest and humble citizens of Smallville, whose virtues instill humility in the Man of Steel and inspire him to champion the common good of all mankind. And for a Superman who has trod the soils of other worlds, nothing is more comforting than walking the well-worn paths of home.

SUPERPOWERS

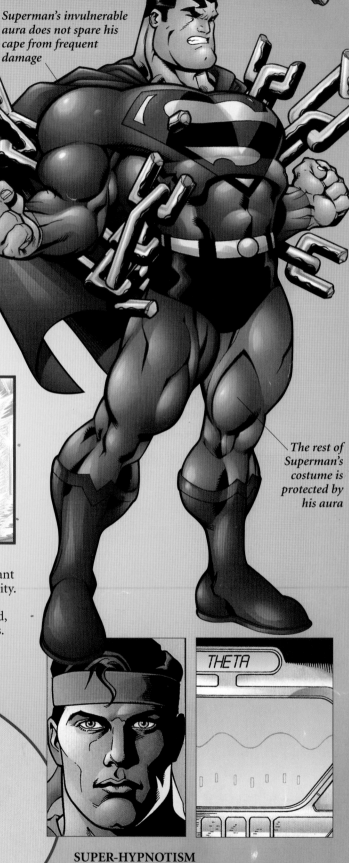

INVISIBLE ARMOR
Superman's invulnerability is the result of an invisible aura that covers his entire body. This force field, generated by his solar-irradiated cells, makes his skin nearly impenetrable. Bullets easily ricochet off the Man of Steel!

THERE IS VERY LITTLE that Superman cannot do. Under the rays of Earth's yellow sun, his Kryptonian cells serve as living solar batteries that fuel a variety of astonishing abilities. He is super-strong, able to divert the course of raging rivers. In Earth's gravity, he possesses the power of flight, traversing great distances at amazing speeds. As well, Superman's senses are magnified far beyond mortal abilities. He can see with telescopic, microscopic, or X-ray vision. His eyes can emit laser-like beams of heat vision. His ears can detect the footfall of an ant. With these great powers come unmatched stamina and virtual invulnerability to injury, making him a true Man of Steel!

Superman's invulnerable aura does not spare his cape from frequent damage

The rest of Superman's costume is protected by his aura

Lois marvels at Superman's heart-stopping aerial acrobatics!

X-RAY VISION
Superman's unique vision allows him to scan distant objects (or microscopic details) with amazing clarity. His so-called X-ray vision permits him to see through all solid objects with the exception of lead, the only substance impervious to his optic powers.

THE POWER OF FLIGHT
He can leap tall buildings with a single bound and soar into the sky like a bird or a plane. Since Earth exerts less gravitational pull than Krypton once did, Superman's solar-powered body flies by his own force of will. The Man of Steel has yet to measure the limits of his flight velocity, though he has easily exceeded the speed of sound, creating ear-shattering sonic booms in his wake.

THETA

SUPER-HYPNOTISM
Though he has yet to master its intricacies, Superman sometimes utilizes the *Torquasm-Vo*, an ancient Kryptonian warrior discipline. By shifting his consciousness onto a higher (Theta) state, he can fight an enemy in a purely mental realm.

HEAT VISION

S.T.A.R. Labs researchers theorize that Superman's heat vision involves complex microwave manipulation. Superman has honed this special ability into an amazing power, capable of projecting gentle warmth or melting sold rock!

SOLAR POWER

When he first landed on Earth, the infant Kal-El was as weak as a human baby. However, prolonged exposure to Earth's yellow sun slowly energized his Kryptonian cells. Young Clark Kent did not manifest his superpowers until his late teens, but in time his solar-charged body fueled a Superman!

Earth's sun remains the wellspring for all of Superman's heroic abilities.

A super-strong fist sends Mongul reeling!

SUPER-STRENGTH

If push came to shove, the Man of Tomorrow might just be able to move a mountain. His crushing grip can certainly wring diamonds from coal! Though not infinite, Superman's strength is suitably staggering. He is more than capable of muscling a robot juggernaut onto the scrap heap, or punching an alien overlord into the stratosphere. Nevertheless, the Man of Steel's strength is tempered by an instinctive control of his formidable might.

SUPER-BREATH

With careful training, the Man of Steel has developed amazing breathing powers. He is able to condense oxygen in his lungs to a pressurized and super-cold state, or hold his breath in outer space for long periods. He can exhale a super-concentrated gust to snuff out blazing fires or flash-freeze violent villains into submission!

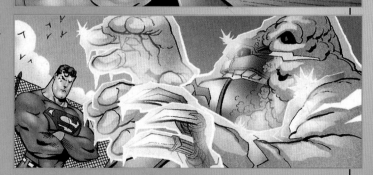

BULLETS MAY BOUNCE off Superman's steel-hard skin, but the Man of Tomorrow isn't totally without an Achilles' heel. He must breathe like any other person, although he is able to store air in his lungs when traveling through outer space. Since his body converts solar energy into superpowers, lack of sunlight will cause his strength to dwindle over time. He is also susceptible to the unpredictable forces of magic and illusion. And most of all, Superman is vulnerable to the deadly radiation of kryptonite, the meteoric remnants from his own home planet!

BREATHING PROBLEMS

Though Mongul II helped Superman to expand his lung capacity, the Man of Steel still requires a high-tech rebreather to survive extended periods without air.

KRYPTONITE

The Green Death that led to Krypton's explosive end continues to torment its sole survivor. When Superman's home planet exploded, its radioactive mantle and core were scattered throughout the universe as green-glowing shards of kryptonite. Exposure to the element will reduce Superman's powers and swiftly kill him. Although all the kryptonite on Earth has been destroyed, poisonous pieces of Superman's past still drift through space.

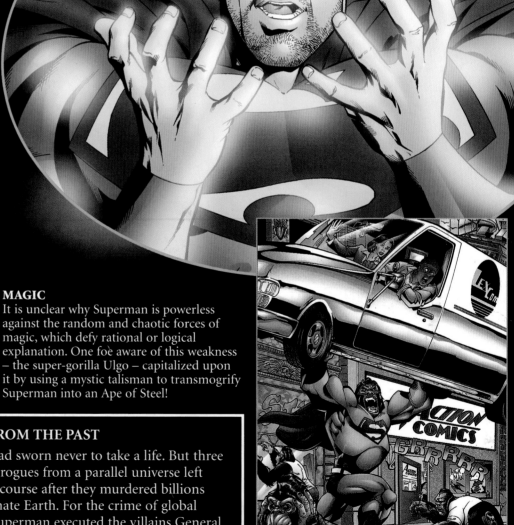

MAGIC

It is unclear why Superman is powerless against the random and chaotic forces of magic, which defy rational or logical explanation. One foe aware of this weakness – the super-gorilla Ulgo – capitalized upon it by using a mystic talisman to transmogrify Superman into an Ape of Steel!

GHOSTS FROM THE PAST

Superman had sworn never to take a life. But three Kryptonian rogues from a parallel universe left him little recourse after they murdered billions on an alternate Earth. For the crime of global genocide, Superman executed the villains General Zod, Faora, and Quex-Ul with kryptonite, an act that still haunts him.

ALL THIS POWER ...

Despite his awesome abilities, the Man of Steel cannot help everyone, nor be everywhere he is needed. Even a Superman can fail, and it is his own fallibility that cuts the Man of Steel to his invulnerable core. He could not save the millions of Topeka, Kansas, during the Imperiex War. And for the billions Superman did save, he still mourns each and every soul he was unable to pluck from harm's way.

I HAVE ALL THIS POWER...

...AND I COULDN'T SAVE THEM...

SUPER-EGO
Dominus saw the potential for psychological warfare in Superman's own self-doubt and manipulated the Last Son of Krypton into declaring himself King of the World! Before he came to his senses, the maddened Man of Steel policed the globe with his own private army of Superman-Robots!

NO!!

hh! hh! hh!

CLARK? WH-WHUSS WRONG?

NIGHTMARES
Occasionally, anxiety over his great responsibilities manifests itself as bad dreams for the Man of Steel. Superman frequently worries about the safety of those he loves and his ability to protect them from the deadly schemes of his many diabolical foes.

SUPER STYLE

THE HEALING SYMBOL
Superman's emblem echoes the design adorning an Iroquois healing blanket that belonged to his ancestors Nathaniel and Mary Glenowen-Kent. The S-shaped symbol represents a snake – a great medicine animal totem to the Iroquois.

HOMEMADE HERO

In the moments after he saved the *Constitution*, Clark Kent knew that there was no turning back. The world wanted and needed a hero. But Clark realized that, for his own peace of mind, there would have to be a clear line of distinction between the man and the Superman. Jonathan Kent remembered the first brightly clad "Mystery Men" of the 1940s, so-called super heroes who paved the way for a Man of Steel. A costume designed by Martha Kent evoked all of that imagery and symbolism in a suit fit for a Superman!

Superman's emblem evokes the power to heal. It is recognized everywhere on Earth ... and even beyond Kal-El's adopted world!

CLARK KENT REVEALED HIS SUPERPOWERS to the world when he rescued the space-plane *Constitution* from a crash landing. To preserve his privacy and protect the lives of those he loved most, Clark needed a secret identity… especially if he was to continue functioning as a hero. Jonathan Kent provided the inspiration. Martha Kent volunteered her sewing skills. And Clark himself designed the stylized S-shield adorning the red, blue, and yellow costume that would identify him to the world as Superman!

SUPERMAN BLUE

When Earth's sun was extinguished by the star-consuming "Sun-Eater," the solar-fueled Man of Steel lost his powers. Attempts to restore his super-abilities altered the Last Son of Krypton into a being of pure energy! To contain his volatile new form, Superman sought the help of Professor Emil Hamilton. The helpful scientist wove a containment suit fitted with micro-circuitry webbing to prevent the energized hero from phasing himself out of existence!

Acting LexCorp CEO Contessa Erica del Portenza provided Professor Hamilton with the advanced polymer fabric for Superman's energy-containment suit.

THE ONLY THING I'M SURE OF IS THAT IF IT DOESN'T WORK...

...SUPERMAN WILL BE LOST TO US FOREVER!

SUPERMAN RED
Before he regained his original superpowers, the energy-based Man of Tomorrow briefly split into *two* Supermen! While Superman Blue was cool and rational, Superman Red was hotheaded and headstrong!

Superman's invulnerable aura does not extend to his crimson cape, which must be mended frequently

BACK IN BLACK
Clad in ebony and tarnished silver, a stubble-faced Superman trapped on the Joker's upside-down, cubed Earth, was a dark reflection of his true self. Vaguely echoing his Kryptonian regenerative bodysuit, this corrupted costume was adorned by wrist and ankle bracelets with which to bind Superman each night in the freakish Arkham Asylum!

SUPERMAN'S COSTUME

Aside from its great symbolic value, there is nothing remarkable about Superman's costume. Separated from its wearer, it is neither bulletproof nor tear-resistant. It is not fire-retardant nor stain repelling. However, when worn by the Man of Steel, this blue, red, and yellow cloth is like a suit of armor, rendered impenetrable by the invulnerable aura that surrounds Superman's entire person!

COLORS OF MOURNING

Even as Earth rejoiced in its salvation from destruction after the terrible Imperiex War, Superman grieved for the multitudes he had been unable to save. Martha Kent responded by making him a costume that allowed the Man of Steel to champion his adopted world while honoring the memory of the conflict's casualties. This suit is less vibrantly colorful than its predecessor, and his emblem is emblazoned upon a black field to symbolize mourning. Yet the hero who wears it still believes he will one day win the never-ending battle against evil.

REAL NAME Kal-El

OCCUPATION Super Hero

BASE Metropolis

HEIGHT 6 ft 3 in **WEIGHT** 225 lb

EYES Blue **HAIR** Black

FIRST APPEARANCE
ACTION COMICS #1
(June 1938)

27

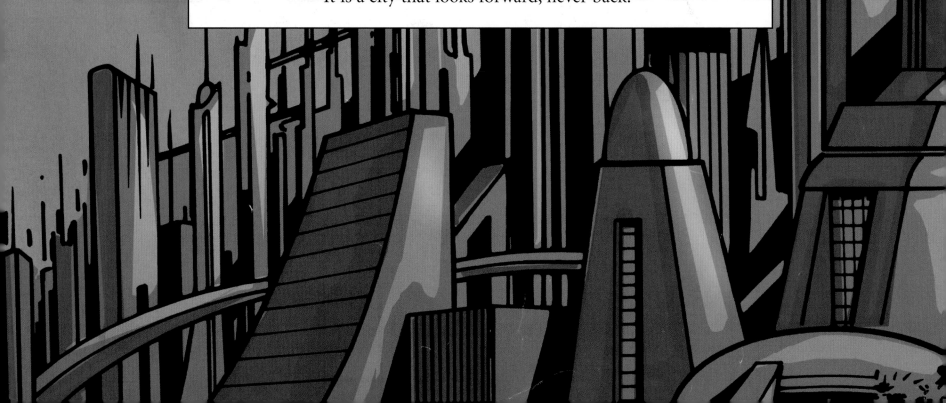

THE CITY OF
TOMORROW

METROPOLIS IS MUCH MORE than a bustling urban center. Like many east coast American cities, Metropolis is a melting pot of peoples and cultures. It is a city of industry. It is a city of ambition. And perhaps most important, it is a City of Tomorrow. It comes as no surprise that Superman chose to make his home here.

With a population almost 11 million citizens strong, Metropolis is as big and exciting as any boy from Smallville, Kansas, could imagine. This city of opportunity gave young Clark Kent his big break – as a reporter on the prestigious *Daily Planet* newspaper. And in those very offices he would find not only lifelong friendship, but true love! Metropolis is a home base for Superman, and it is also a city with its own unique problems. It needs a helping hand. Both driven by and dependent upon Lex Luthor for its economic well-being, Metropolis also faces the constant threat of alien attacks and super-villain strikes. Despite all that, Metropolis is a city in which optimism shines through. It is a city that looks forward, never back.

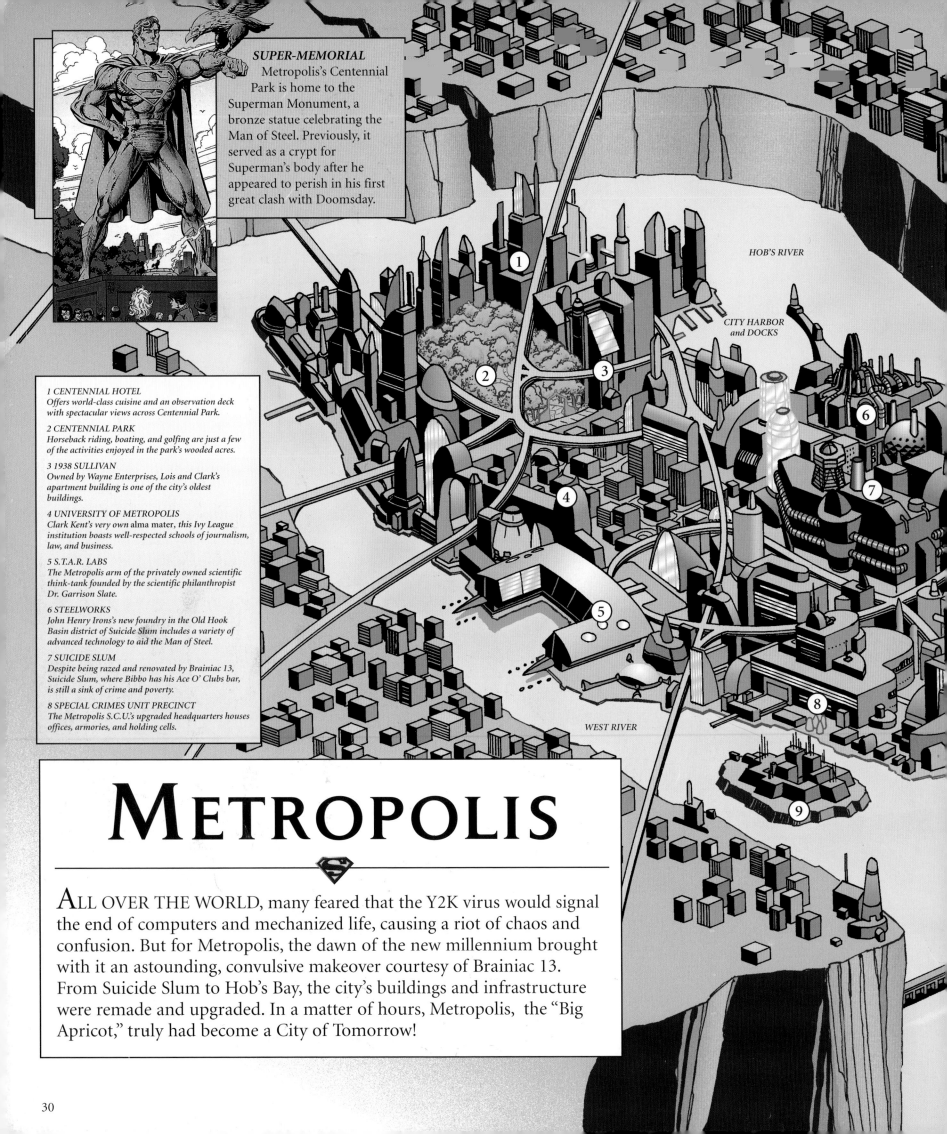

HOB'S RIVER

CITY HARBOR and DOCKS

1 CENTENNIAL HOTEL
Offers world-class cuisine and an observation deck with spectacular views across Centennial Park.

2 CENTENNIAL PARK
Horseback riding, boating, and golfing are just a few of the activities enjoyed in the park's wooded acres.

3 1938 SULLIVAN
Owned by Wayne Enterprises, Lois and Clark's apartment building is one of the city's oldest buildings.

4 UNIVERSITY OF METROPOLIS
Clark Kent's very own alma mater, this Ivy League institution boasts well-respected schools of journalism, law, and business.

5 S.T.A.R. LABS
The Metropolis arm of the privately owned scientific think-tank founded by the scientific philanthropist Dr. Garrison Slate.

6 STEELWORKS
John Henry Irons's new foundry in the Old Hook Basin district of Suicide Slum includes a variety of advanced technology to aid the Man of Steel.

7 SUICIDE SLUM
Despite being razed and renovated by Brainiac 13, Suicide Slum, where Bibbo has his Ace O' Clubs bar, is still a sink of crime and poverty.

8 SPECIAL CRIMES UNIT PRECINCT
The Metropolis S.C.U.'s upgraded headquarters houses offices, armories, and holding cells.

WEST RIVER

METROPOLIS

ALL OVER THE WORLD, many feared that the Y2K virus would signal the end of computers and mechanized life, causing a riot of chaos and confusion. But for Metropolis, the dawn of the new millennium brought with it an astounding, convulsive makeover courtesy of Brainiac 13. From Suicide Slum to Hob's Bay, the city's buildings and infrastructure were remade and upgraded. In a matter of hours, Metropolis, the "Big Apricot," truly had become a City of Tomorrow!

BOROUGHS OF METROPOLIS

Situated on an island separated from the mainland by Hob's River to the north and the West River to the south, Metropolis is a city that has never quite outgrown its "expansion phase." New Troy encompasses the urban boroughs of the island itself. Park Ridge and its subdivisions are Metropolis's oldest suburbs, while Bakerline is home to the city's middle class. Only the wealthiest can afford the oceanfront real estate of St. Martin's Island and Hell's Gate, and Queensland Park is home to the city's growing immigrant populace.

While Brainiac 13's technology was infused throughout Metropolis, the city's infrastructure literally repaired itself, like the self-rebuilding tracks of the triple-decker "Rail Whale" commuter train seen here.

9 STRYKER'S ISLAND PENITENTIARY
The ultimate maximum security prison possesses high-tech detention facilities designed to accommodate the most powerful metahuman villains.

10 UNION STATION
Located in the heart of the city, Union Station links the national railroad network to Metropolis's unique "Rail Whale" commuter grid.

11 METROPOLIS CITY HOSPITAL
This state-of-the-art medical center maintains a privileges-sharing program with S.T.A.R. Labs.

12 JULES VERNE EXTRA-TERRESTRIAL MUSEUM
The museum exhibits artifacts from alien worlds and presents guest lectures by interplanetary heroes.

13 LENA LUTHOR SCIENCE EXPLORARIUM
Technological advances abound in this interactive museum named after Luthor's infant daughter.

14 CITY HALL
The administrative center of Metropolis has mayoral, governmental, and emergency services offices.

15 S.A.I. DAM
Hydroelectric waterworks control the flow of twin rivers and the recycling of the city reservoir.

16 HYPERSECTOR
The business and financial center of Metropolis.

17 HOTEL METROPOLIS
Five-star luxury accommodation located amid the heart of Downtown.

18 SHUSTER HALL
Metropolis's premier theater has been in service since 1938.

19 GBS BUILDING
The corporate hub of Galaxy Communications' media conglomerate.

20 DAILY PLANET BUILDING
The home of the respected, globally circulated newspaper, Metropolis's oldest and most beloved publication. The Daily Planet Building with its distinctive hologram globe is one of the city's most famous landmarks.

21 METROPOLIS MUSEUM OF ART
Galleries include important historical and contemporary artistic works.

22 LEXCORP TOWERS
Designed to form a double L, Lex Luthor's 307-story citadels are not only Metropolis's highest buildings, but the tallest skyscraper in the world! Its defense systems include robot sentries and mutable glass windows.

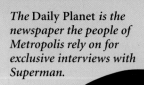

The Daily Planet *is the newspaper the people of Metropolis rely on for exclusive interviews with Superman.*

THE DAILY PLANET

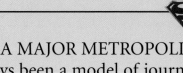

AS A MAJOR METROPOLITAN NEWSPAPER, the *Daily Planet* has always been a model of journalistic integrity. Just as the holographic globe atop the Daily Planet Building shines forth as a beacon in the Metropolis skyline, the publication illuminates the news of the day with hard-hitting and award-winning reporting. It was the *Daily Planet* that first revealed Superman's existence to the world. Years later, the paper – published by veteran editor Perry White and staffed by acclaimed reporters Lois Lane, Ron Troupe, Dirk Armstrong, and Clark Kent – continues to chronicle the adventures of Superman.

DON'T CALL HIM "CHIEF"!

Perry White has held practically every position at the *Daily Planet*. Starting out as a newsboy in Suicide Slum, Perry climbed the paper's ranks, from copy boy to top reporter, eventually becoming editor-in-chief and publisher. After nearly five decades, he now has a controlling interest in the newspaper to which he has dedicated himself.

BUSY OFFICE

The *Daily Planet* has changed much since it was founded in 1775 by American colonial patriot Joshua Merriweather. What began as the weekly tract *Our Planet* has grown into one of the world's leading periodicals, published twice daily – morning and evening – and reprinted in several foreign-language editions.

THE A-TEAM

Eschewing the business-burdened role of publisher, *Daily Planet* Editor-in-Chief Perry White prefers instead to get his hands dirty with inky newsprint. From his well-worn desk, White manages one of the most well-respected reporting teams in the world, including Pulitzer Prize-winning investigative journalist Lois Lane and her husband, foreign correspondent Clark Kent, secretly the *Planet*'s headline-making Man of Steel!

CAT GRANT

The *Planet*'s former gossip columnist and later host of her own WGBS-TV chat show, Catherine "Cat" Grant has recently risen to the lofty post of Press Secretary for President Lex Luthor! Cat struggled with and overcame alcoholism after her son Adam was murdered by the Toyman. She hopes her tenure in the White House signals a new beginning in her life.

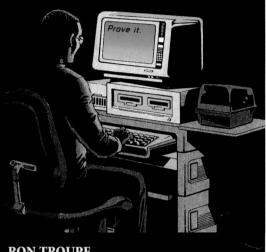

RON TROUPE

Ron Troupe's poignant reporting of Superman's tragic battle with Doomsday earned him a permanent spot on the *Planet*'s staff. Ron is married to Lois Lane's sister, Lucy and they have a son named Sam, after Lucy's father, the late General Samuel Lane.

Y2K REBUILD

Like every other edifice in the city, the Daily Planet Building was structurally upgraded by Brainiac 13's millennial assault on Metropolis. The 37-story skyscraper housing the *Planet*'s offices is now both sleeker and more user-friendly to its many employees. The *Daily Planet* globe, a Metropolis landmark, was even replaced by a high-tech hologram. The latest technology has afforded the *Planet* greater speed and ease in publishing the stories of the day, and the venerable periodical continues to compete with LexCom and other internet news services as the 21st century unfolds.

OFFICES ATTACKED

The power of the press can move people to action and effect social change. But when Perry White penned a piece expressing his views on the use of Metropolis's leftover Brainiac 13 technology, angry Suicide Slum residents, calling themselves the "Cult of Persuasion," wrecked the *Planet* newsroom with fire-axes! Superman stopped their rampage and rescued the veteran newshound, who still believes that the pen is mightier than the sword.

WHATRE YOU STANDING AROUND FOR?? WE'VE GOT A **PAPER** TO GET OUT!

THE LAST WORD

Work at the *Planet* isn't over until "The Bulldog" – the day's final edition – is "put to bed," with all text sent to the printing presses in the bowels of the Daily Planet Building. Of course, that's when work on the next day's newspaper begins!

CLARK KENT

HE LIKES PEANUT BUTTER AND JELLY sandwiches, a good football game, and the smell of spring in Kansas. He is a writer of modest fame, hoping one day to author the Great American Novel. He is a son, a friend, and a husband. And the best-kept secret on Earth is that Clark Kent is a strange visitor from another planet. While Superman is a public symbol of courage and heroism, this mild-mannered reporter from Smallville is the real man behind the stalwart Man of Steel.

MILD-MANNERED REPORTER

Clark left Smallville to travel the world while his powers developed. He revealed himself as Superman by saving Lois Lane and the space-plane *Constitution*. Clark reported the story himself, scooping Lane and becoming the *Daily Planet*'s newest journalist!

With glasses to disguise his heroic profile, Clark enrolls at Metropolis University!

REAL NAME
Clark Joseph Kent

OCCUPATION
Foreign Correspondent

BASE Metropolis

HEIGHT 6 ft 3 in **WEIGHT** 225 lb

EYES Blue **HAIR** Black

FIRST APPEARANCE
ACTION COMICS #1
(June 1938)

THE INSIDE STORY

After his sojourn abroad, Clark Kent attended Metropolis University, where journalism became his major course of study. Clark was drawn to the printed word and the power it wielded. After graduating and securing employment at the *Daily Planet*, Clark hoped to control the public perception of Superman, if only through the stories he reported from an "insider's perspective."

OFFICE ROMANCE

In the beginning, Lois Lane bristled at her fellow reporter Clark Kent. After all, Clark beat her to the story of a lifetime. At first fiercely competitive, the *Daily Planet*'s top two reporters soon grew closer. But Lois was also attracted to Superman and to other musclebound potential suitors. Clark realized that revealing his secret was perhaps inevitable if he were to win her heart.

TRUTH AND JUSTICE

At first, news reporting afforded Clark a more thorough indoctrination into the ways of mankind. But the free press also taught him the power of truth, a moral value first instilled in him by the Kents, and as essential to a Man of Steel as super-strength or heat vision. Even though Superman could free an innocent man by bending open the steel bars of his prison cell, the press could be an even more potent force in ferreting out the evidence necessary to exonerate the falsely accused!

Clark Kent's investigative reporting benefits from his all-seeing and truth-revealing X-ray vision!

LANA...?!

LOIS...?

LANA LANG

She was Clark's first love and closest childhood friend, a red-haired beauty privy to Clark's super-secret for many years. Lana married fellow Smallville chum Pete Ross. Lana and Pete owe the life of their son, Clark Peter Ross, to Superman, who once saved the baby from Brainiac's insidious clutches!

THE BIG SECRET

Clark Kent now serves the *Daily Planet* as a foreign correspondent, making it far easier for him to become the Man of Steel when a crisis looms. Prior to holding this more flexible position, Clark used to slip away from his desk on the flimsiest of pretexts and head for the privacy of a secluded storeroom, there to shed his street clothes and become Superman.

LOIS LANE

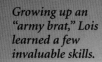

Growing up an "army brat," Lois learned a few invaluable skills.

MEETING THE MAN OF STEEL changed her life. Already a Pulitzer Prize-winning journalist, Lois Lane had reported from the front lines of war zones and natural catastrophes. But the biggest scoop of Lois's career came when she looked out the portal of a plummeting space-plane and witnessed a miracle. She dubbed her savior "Superman." To her annoyance, she was beaten to the exclusive by a rookie reporter named Clark Kent. Lois then found her affections torn between gentle Clark and heroic Superman. How could *she* know the two men were one and the same?!

LIFE IN THE FAST LANE

Lois Lane has often topped Metropolis's "Best Dressed" list. A reporter's salary doesn't run to a sports car, but Lois can thank Lex Luthor for her red Lamborghini, a wedding gift from the mogul.

REAL NAME
Lois Joanne Lane

OCCUPATION Reporter

BASE Metropolis

HEIGHT 5 ft 6 in **WEIGHT** 120 lb

EYES Blue **HAIR** Auburn

FIRST APPEARANCE
ACTION COMICS #1
(June 1938)

TOP REPORTER

While still in her teens, Lois impressed *Daily Planet* Managing Editor Perry White by smuggling an incriminating document out of LexCorp headquarters. In time, Lois became the *Planet*'s most skilful investigative reporter. Lois is an author of note, with several mystery novels to her credit as well.

I GOT IT, PERRY.

LOVE AT FIRST SIGHT?

As a guest aboard the experimental space-plane *Constitution*, Lois expected a routine flight. Instead, she met her guardian angel when the aircraft plunged from the sky!

Lois has some trouble with a Superman robot.

SURVIVAL SKILLS

The eldest daughter of a career military man, Lois was raised to be tough as nails. At an early age she was schooled in survival training and hand-to-hand combat skills while living on the succession of U. S. Army bases to which her father, Sam Lane, was assigned.

Even with her hands bound, Lois Lane knows how to fight back!

TEMPER, TEMPER!

As a child, Lois endured the strict discipline and frequent criticism of Sam Lane, who made it no secret that he would have preferred sons. Lois learned to stand up for herself early on. Never one to back down from a conflict, she does not suffer fools lightly.

LUCY LANE

Falling victim to blindness in adulthood drove Lois's younger sister Lucy to attempt suicide while visiting Lois in Metropolis. Saved by the first Bizarro Superman, Lucy regained her vision after the imperfect duplicate's atomized remains sprinkled into her sightless eyes. Lucy briefly dated Jimmy Olsen, before falling in love with and marrying *Daily Planet* reporter Ron Troupe.

POSSESSED!

In the company of Superman, Lois Lane has seen some very strange things. But Viroxx was like no other, an alien virus that infested Lois and turned her against the Man of Steel, Earth, and the entire universe! As a mindless brood-leader, Lois prepared new worlds to share her fate before Superman freed her from Viroxx's thrall!

GENERAL SAM LANE

Lois's father ascended to the penultimate military post in the land when Lex Luthor took office as President of the United States. Named to Luthor's cabinet as Secretary of Defense, General Sam Lane coordinated the U.S.-led forces defending Earth against Imperiex.

THE WAR HERO

General Sam Lane lived and died a soldier. Lois watched from the presidential war-room as Lane, commanding a tank brigade, defended the White House from an Imperiex-Probe. He sacrificed his own life to stop the probe's unrelenting advance by igniting his tank's nuclear engine.

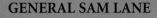

THE ONLY WAY TO FLY!

When she first glimpsed her strange visitor from another planet, Lois quickly came to believe that a man could fly. Soon, the jet-setting journalist was floating with the Man of Steel, sharing first his secrets, then his adventures, and later his life. The woman who has lived on nearly every continent now vacations in such otherworldly locales as the trans-dimensional world of Kandor, happy to soar alongside the love she calls "Superman."

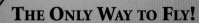

SUDDEN DEATH

A THUNDEROUS CLASH OF TITANS shook Metropolis to its very foundations. When it was all over, there was only silence. To stop the unstoppable Doomsday, Superman had pursued the raging creature through a swath of mindless destruction ending in his beloved city. Even as Doomsday defeated his comrades in the Justice League of America, a broken and bloody Man of Steel would not yield! With his last remaining breath, the Last Son of Krypton toppled the mighty monster. And as the dust settled, Metropolis could do nothing but mourn its fallen Superman.

THE BATTLE RAGES!

The Man of Steel and the "Armageddon Creature" were evenly matched …When the invulnerable Superman struck the equally indestructible Doomsday, he did little damage to the monster. But with its bony spurs and razor-sharp extrusions, Doomsday was able to pierce Superman's skin and draw Kryptonian blood!

MOVE IN CLOSER! WE'RE BROADCASTING THIS LIVE!

A CITY IN RUINS
Superman's battle with Doomsday threatened to raze Metropolis! The city's streets shattered to rubble as vehicles were tossed around like toys. Even U.S. Army troops armed with Cadmus Project shock cannons could not halt Doomsday's rampage!

DEATH BLOW

As the battle reached its crescendo, their final punches echoed like shock waves through the skyscraper canyons of Metropolis. Superman used his dwindling strength to stop Doomsday once and for all. But the creature's final blow also proved the Man of Steel's undoing.

THE FALLEN HERO

The dying Man of Steel lay in the arms of his one true love. Shocked Metropolitans and members of the Justice League wept openly as Lois Lane cradled Superman's body and prayed for a miracle. But it was too late …

FUNERAL FOR A FRIEND

It seemed as if the sky itself were crying the day Superman was laid to rest in Metropolis. On a cold and rainy morning, Superman's funeral procession attracted thousands of citizens determined to pay their final respects. The JLA was there. So were the Metal Men, Outsiders, and every other hero and heroine inspired by the Man of Tomorrow. All wore armbands of mourning as Superman's body was carried to its resting place in Centennial Park. There, beneath a golden statue of the fallen hero, the legend of Superman would endure even beyond death.

THE RETURI!

COULD THE MAN OF TOMORROW really be dead? The sudden appearance of *four* Supermen suggested otherwise. One was a Man of Steel hoping to provide Metropolis with the living hero it desperately needed. Another was a brash super-powered teen who claimed to be Kal-El's clone. A third – an emotionless, enigmatic figure – declared he was the resurrected Last Son of Krypton. But all other claims were disputed by a Cyborg-Superman who possessed Kryptonian DNA!

BODY-SNATCHED!
Skeptical of the mysterious Men of Steel soaring over Metropolis, Lois Lane and Police Chief William Henderson investigated Superman's crypt in Centennial Park. Beneath the bronze memorial to the Man of Steel they found an empty coffin and a tunnel leading to the cloning facilities of Project Cadmus!

CYBORG

STEEL

THE ERADICATOR

SUPERBOY

THE IMPOSTER OF STEEL
Half-man, half-machine, the Cyborg-Superman had everyone fooled. In reality, he was Hank Henshaw, an astronaut whose body had been destroyed by cosmic radiation and converted into pure energy. Believing the Man of Steel responsible for his own fate and also the death of his wife, Henshaw devised a new form for himself using Kal-El's Kryptonian genetic template. But impersonating Superman was only the beginning of his revenge …

REIGN OF THE SUPERMEN
Each of the four Men of Steel seemed authentic, but none possessed Superman's superpowers. The Cyborg's bionic parts reflected superior Kryptonian technology. Steel's armor enabled his feats of super-strength. The Eradicator wielded bizarre energy blasts. Superboy relied on "tactile-telekinesis" to prove his mettle!

WHO WEARS THE WARSUIT?
Allied with Mongul, the Cyborg obliterated California's Coast City and replaced it with Engine City, a propulsion unit designed to turn Earth into a new Warworld! Meanwhile, a Kryptonian Warsuit climbed out of Metropolis's Hob's Bay. But who was piloting the juggernaut?

KRWHAM!

As Lois Lane, Lex Luthor, Supergirl, Superboy, and Steel watched, the Kryptonian Warsuit disgorged its mysterious occupant … SUPERMAN!

THE ERADICATOR'S SACRIFICE

The one true Man of Steel could not have returned from death's dominion without the intervention of the Eradicator, who transported Superman's lifeless body to the Fortress of Solitude. There, Kal-El was placed in a Kryptonian rejuvenation chamber that resuscitated and healed him!

HE'S BACK!

Though his powers were not yet fully restored, the Man of Steel – joined by Supergirl, Green Lantern, and the three remaining Supermen – launched an assault upon Engine City. Mongul's forces were routed, but the Eradicator, whose prime directive was to preserve Kryptonian life, sacrificed himself to shield Superman from the Cyborg's last-ditch kryptonite attack. In the end, the Cyborg was seemingly destroyed and the world rejoiced in Superman's return.

TOGETHER AGAIN

As the surviving heroes mopped up the remains of Engine City and Mongul's hordes, Superman rocketed home to Metropolis. Lois awoke from a fitful sleep to find him floating at her window. Faster than a speeding bullet, the two lovers embraced, knowing at long last that not even death could keep them apart.

LOIS & CLARK

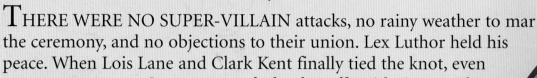

THERE WERE NO SUPER-VILLAIN attacks, no rainy weather to mar the ceremony, and no objections to their union. Lex Luthor held his peace. When Lois Lane and Clark Kent finally tied the knot, even Superman took the day off! With Jimmy Olsen serving as best man and Lucy Lane standing as maid of honor, Lois and Clark exchanged their solemn vows, pledging their undying love for one another, as friends and family celebrated their long-awaited marriage.

PARTNERS ON THE PLANET

Initially, Clark Kent worried over Lois Lane's attraction to his alter ego, the Man of Steel. But working closely with Clark at the *Daily Planet* made Lois appreciate the reality of her caring co-worker much more than the fantasy of flying with a Superman.

OLSEN! LANE! KENT! MY OFFICE NOW!

YOU'RE A STUBBORN, OPINIONATED WOMAN, LOIS LANE.

WILL YOU MARRY ME?

CLARK PROPOSES

At first the independent, irrepressible Lois turned Clark down, fearing she might lose her individuality as "Mrs. Superman."

JUST MARRIED!

After a brawl during Clark's bachelor party at Bibbo's Ace O' Clubs bar, the happy couple were married at 2:30 p.m. on June 19 in the Metropolis Chapel of United Faiths. The wedding was everything Lois and Clark dreamed it would be, a quiet ceremony surrounded by only their closest loved ones. Jealous Lex Luthor eavesdropped on the nuptials via closed-circuit TV!

KRYPTO CHAOS

Some say pet ownership is a married couple's first step towards parenthood. Lois Lane would beg to differ. When a Kryptonian canine followed the super-couple home through the Phantom Zone, Lois allowed her husband to keep the rambunctious "Krypto," not realizing that the alien dog would also be super-powered!

After tearing Lois and Clark's apartment to shreds, Krypto now resides in the Fortress of Solitude.

THE WEIGHT OF THE WORLD

Superman's doubts about his ability to safeguard Earth from its own self-destruction allowed the mind-altering Dominus to drive a wedge between the Man of Steel and humanity. But Lois didn't give up on her heroic husband. All it took was a kiss more real than the world of fear Dominus created.

1938 SULLIVAN

Lois and Clark live in a spacious rent-controlled apartment in 1938 Sullivan, one of the oldest domiciles in Metropolis. Interestingly, the building itself is owned by billionaire Bruce Wayne, secretly the Batman! Living with Clark can be a mite trying at times, but at least he's handy around the home!

SOUL MATES

Together, Lois and Clark are an almost perfect match. Even before marriage, Lois knew that she would have to share her Superman with the world, through good times and bad, the inevitable alien attacks and the uncertainty of his never-ending battle against injustice. However in Clark she found a man who was supportive and not intimidated by her having her own life and career. As for Clark, he remains grounded in a love stronger even than a Man of Steel!

JIMMY OLSEN

SUPERMAN'S PAL is James Bartholomew Olsen. But to his fellow staff members at the *Daily Planet*, he's just plain "Jimmy." As a news intern, Jimmy befriended reporter Clark Kent and his alter ego Superman, each of whom inspired the cub reporter to seek out adventure. Over the years, Jimmy has held many jobs, from Turtle Boy cartoon pitchman to WGBS television journalist, but this self-styled "Mr. Action" knows the job he loves most is news photographer for the *Daily Planet*, where he's always close to at least *one* of his best friends!

ACTION FIGURE

Superman is a big brother and surrogate parent to Jimmy, whose own father, a covert military operative, went missing in action just after Jimmy's birth. Sarah Olsen raised Jimmy in Metropolis's Bakerline district. She was dismayed when her highly intelligent son abandoned academic life for more thrilling pursuits.

DANGEROUS PURSUITS

It's not easy being Superman's friend and a trainee reporter. Frequently, Jimmy's worlds collide, landing him in a heap of trouble! The demoness Blaze, geneticists Simyan and Mokkari, and the crime cartel Intergang (right) are just a few of the enemies eager to put Olsen out of action!

GAHH~!

SKREEE

Daily Planet *Chief Perry White, determined to make a newspaperman out of Jimmy, lectures the young reporter on the importance of photographs guaranteeing truth in journalism.*

REAL NAME
James Bartholomew Olsen
OCCUPATION Photographer
BASE Metropolis
HEIGHT 5 ft 7 in WEIGHT 140 lb
EYES Blue HAIR Red
FIRST APPEARANCE
SUPERMAN vol. 1 #13
(November 1941)

ZEEEEE ZEE EEE

CALLING SUPERMAN!

As well as having a keen photographic eye, Jimmy is a whiz at electronics. Concealed in his "signal watch" is a microchip beacon to alert the Man of Steel whenever Jimmy needs help. This hypersonic transmitter is audible only to Superman's super-sensitive ears.

Jimmy stole a kiss from Supergirl when she rescued him from Bizarro's clutches.

A TEENAGER IN LOVE

Jimmy has never been lucky in love. He dated Lois Lane's sister Lucy, but the romance didn't last, and he flirted fruitlessly with the beautiful, but mischief-making Misa, one of the Cadmus Project's superhuman "Hairies." And when he met the new incarnation of Supergirl it was love at first sight – but, alas, *only* for Jimmy!

Misa was even more of a "wild child" than Jimmy, especially with her high-tech bag of gadgets!

MEEARGHH!

Strangely enough, the bite of the snapping super-hero "Turtle" combined chemically with honey-dijon mustard in Jimmy's bloodstream to turn him into a titanic tortoise!

THE GREAT TRANSFORMER

While trapped on the Joker's "Bizarro World," Jimmy became Gravedigger Lad, groundskeeper to Bizarro #1's macabre "Graveyard of Solitude." Later, Jimmy suffered further humiliation by being turned into a giant Turtle Boy like his former television persona!

45

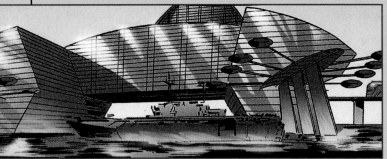

S.T.A.R. Labs

ONLY THE BRIGHTEST MINDS are employed by Scientific and Technological Advanced Research Laboratories. Despite boasting cutting-edge complexes in nearly every major city in the United States and across the globe, S.T.A.R. Labs' Metropolis facility is its most ambitious "think-tank." Whether developing alternative energy sources or mapping the super-human metagene, S.T.A.R. Labs is dedicated to discovery and frequently aids the Man of Steel by providing personnel and equipment to help safeguard Metropolis.

BRANCH BEGINNINGS

S.T.A.R. Labs was founded in Metropolis by the altruistic Dr. Garrison Slate, a scientist who envisioned a chain of nonprofit, experimental workshops free of governmental constraints. Relocated to the West Side Harbor, S.T.A.R. Labs Metropolis now occupies an innovative structure provided by Lex Luthor.

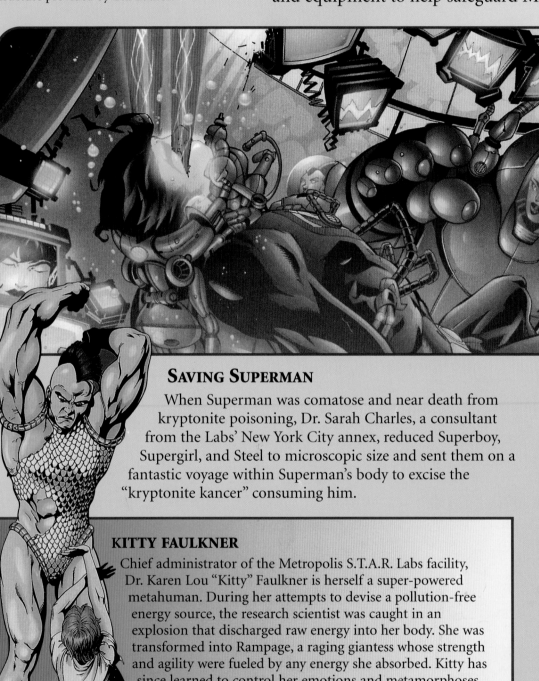

KITTY FAULKNER

SAVING SUPERMAN

When Superman was comatose and near death from kryptonite poisoning, Dr. Sarah Charles, a consultant from the Labs' New York City annex, reduced Superboy, Supergirl, and Steel to microscopic size and sent them on a fantastic voyage within Superman's body to excise the "kryptonite kancer" consuming him.

KITTY FAULKNER

Chief administrator of the Metropolis S.T.A.R. Labs facility, Dr. Karen Lou "Kitty" Faulkner is herself a super-powered metahuman. During her attempts to devise a pollution-free energy source, the research scientist was caught in an explosion that discharged raw energy into her body. She was transformed into Rampage, a raging giantess whose strength and agility were fueled by any energy she absorbed. Kitty has since learned to control her emotions and metamorphoses.

When she mutates into Rampage, Dr. Kitty Faulkner's body converts energy into additional muscle mass.

PROFESSOR HAMILTON

Though not employed by S.T.A.R. Labs, Professor Emil Hamilton is granted access to the facility's equipment and annexes as a trusted consultant. The professor once worked for LexCorp, but he left that company's service when his patents were perverted to Lex Luthor's evil ends. Perhaps for that very reason, the professor has become one of Superman's closest friends, a garrulous genius who prides himself on his knowledge and understanding of the Man of Steel.

Professor Hamilton repairs a damaged Superman-Robot.

MECHANICAL MENACE

Hamilton possesses an artificial limb, a cybernetic prosthesis he built to replace his lost left arm. When Brainiac 13 upgraded Metropolis's technology with his spider-like nanobots, the Professor's cyber-arm was also transmoded. Consequently, Hamilton has unfortunately evolved into the Overmind, leader of a gang of techno-criminals known as the Cybermoths.

RESEARCHERS-IN-RESIDENCE

Kitty Faulkner frequently shares research with fellow bio-radiological expert Professor Bridgette Crosby, a member of the S.T.A.R. Labs team that worked feverishly to save Superman from kryptonite poisoning. While all Earthly kryptonite has since been eliminated, Dr. Crosby now focuses her studies on developing an anti-serum for the lethal green-glowing element.

PROJECT CADMUS

DOC ANGEL
Dr. Helen Angelico is a respected practitioner of metahuman medicine. She first came to Cadmus to treat Superboy for a clone malady that robbed him of his powers.

IT IS THE WORLD'S foremost genetics research facility. Maintained by the U.S. government, the top-secret Project Cadmus is funded solely for the study of cloning. Superboy, the DNAlien Dubbilex, and the resurrected Guardian and Newsboy Legion are all results of the Project's genetic manipulation. Despite such successes, Project Cadmus has also suffered its share of failures, inadvertently gene-splicing more than a few catastrophic creatures. Recently restructured and moved to a secret location, the Project now aims to put its knowledge of genetic science to more practical uses.

SERLING ROQUETTE
Despite being just 16 years old, Dr. Serling Roquette is light-years ahead of most researchers in the study of recombinant DNA. Cadmus's youngest scientist, nicknamed "Doc Rocket," has been an invaluable addition to the Project. Her eclectic tastes in clothing and music are balanced by a maturity and competence far beyond her years.

MICKEY CANNON
In Metropolis's Suicide Slum, Cannon became known as "The Mechanic" for his ability to repair almost anything. This talent later served him well as a government agent. He is now Cadmus's current Director-in-Chief, his presence announced by the clanking of his metal leg brace.

GUARDIAN
During the 1940s, Metropolis's most recognizable masked "Mystery Man" was the Guardian, the costumed alter-ego of policeman Jim Harper. Many years later, the dying Harper was given a new lease on life when Cadmus transferred his consciousness into a healthy cloned body. Guardian repaid the Project by becoming its Security Chief.

Guardian speeds into action aboard the Whiz Wagon, a flying car with a turbo-fusion engine!

DUBBILEX
Given life by Dabney Donovan, the gentle, thoughtful Dubbilex was the first of the so-called DNAliens. His telepathic and telekinetic powers enable him to read minds and mentally move objects. Formerly a mentor to Superboy, Dubbilex is now Cadmus's Head of Genetics.

COLONEL WINTERBOURNE
For nearly a year, Colonel Adam Winterbourne was enslaved by the snake-man Sacker on an uncharted tropical island known as the "Wild Lands." After Superboy liberated Winterbourne, this career soldier requested reassignment to Cadmus, where his experience with genetically altered beasts makes him an ideal military liaison.

SIMYAN AND MOKKARI

Monster-makers in Darkseid's employ, Simyan and Mokkari work tirelessly in their subterranean "Evil Factory" to create genetic abominations. Previously answering to Morgan Edge – Darkseid's Earthly lieutenant and head of Intergang – Simyan and Mokkari are now mostly autonomous, creating freakish beasts and letting them loose upon Cadmus and Metropolis.

NEWSBOY LEGION

Decades ago, Big Words, Scrapper, Gabby, Tommy, and Flip were known as the "Newsboy Legion" in Suicide Slum. As adults, the quintet became department heads at Project Cadmus and were compelled to clone youthful doubles of themselves by the Apokoliptian agent Sleez!

DABNEY DONOVAN

Once the U.S. government's official "mad scientist," Cadmus co-founder Donovan has repeatedly cloned new bodies for himself, lacks any scintilla of scientific ethics, and continues to create dangerous DNAliens to undermine the Project.

DNANGELS

Bioengineered by the U.S. military at a cost of over $2 billion, the DNAngels are a trio of agents first activated to steal the infant clone of Jim Harper from his protector, Superboy. The Angels shared abilities include telekinesis, flight, and bodily transformation.

SERAPH

CHERUB

EPIPHANY

RIPJAK

The British police enlisted Cadmus to discover the identity of history's most notorious serial killer: Jack the Ripper. However, Dabney Donovan stole the Ripper's dried blood sample and created his own flaming demon from hell: Ripjak! Guardian helped defeat the murderous clone before the explosive pyro-granulite Donovan had implanted in its blood reached incendiary critical mass!

SUPER-BABYSITTER

When Guardian was killed by the super-villain Shrapnel, whose power turned him into a living fragmentation bomb, nearly every staff member at Cadmus lamented Jim Harper's death. Superboy was stunned to discover that Harper had been reborn in a new cloned body – and that he was left holding the baby!

SUPERBOY

THE KID KNOWN AS "Superboy" was born in a test tube, created by Project Cadmus in an attempt to replace Superman! Unable to clone Kryptonian DNA, Cadmus geneticists made the next best thing, using cell samples from Project Director Paul Westfield. Cadmus' homegrown hero was designed to mimic Superman's powers. However, the clone was "birthed" before he had fully developed, thus unleashing a young headstrong hero very different from the one Cadmus intended!

The Kid gives Guardian a lift with his tactile-telekinesis

A BOY BY NAME …

Fearing Westfield would misuse his duplicate Superman, the Newsboys prematurely freed the clone. Later, treatment for cellular degeneration temporarily "froze" Superboy's age at 16 years. Fortunately, that side effect wore off and the Kid – given the Kryptonian name "Kon-El" by Superman – now matures normally.

SCREEEECH

SUPERPOWERS

Superboy's superpowers are achieved through genetically engineered "tactile-telekinesis" which grants him flight, super-strength, and the ability to disassemble any objects he touches. Sadly, Superboy also inherited a vulnerability to kryptonite.

King Shark takes a bite of Superboy!

SUPER-FOES

Although he has only been alive a few years, Superboy has already accumulated a large rogues gallery of meta-villains eager to cut short his clone life! Black Zero, a renegade Superboy from a parallel universe known as "Hypertime-Earth," takes his name from the Kryptonian anti-cloning terrorist group. The man-fish Nanaue, a.k.a. King Shark, may have been a tragic mutation, or – as Hawaiian legend would have it – the spawn of a mortal woman and a Shark God!

Black Zero zaps the Kid with heat vision!

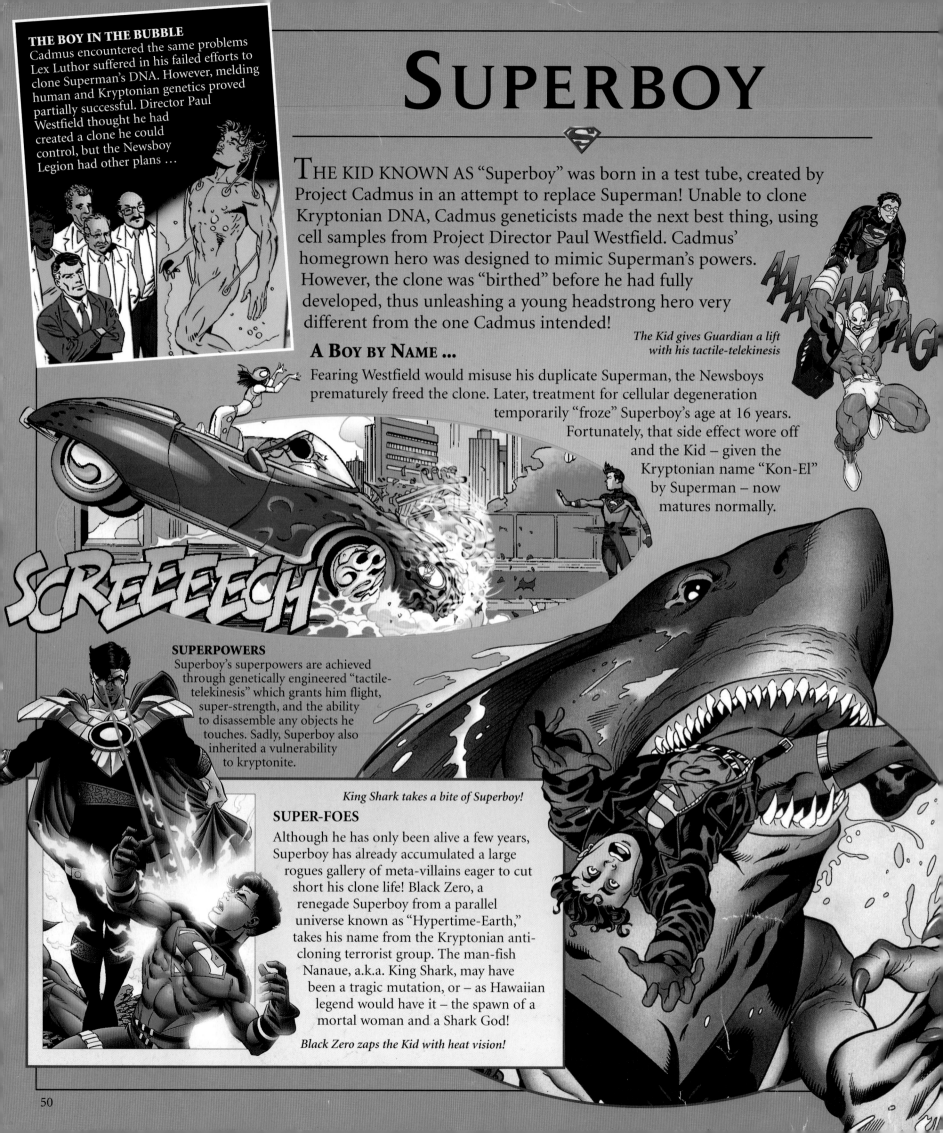

KNOCKOUT

A young Female Fury from Apokolips, the hard-hitting Knockout left a lasting impression on the Kid, whom she affectionately called "Pup." Superboy was convinced he could reform the beguiling beauty, who succeeded in turning him against his closest friends for a time. Unfortunately, Knockout is not one to be spurned.

REAL NAME Kon-El

OCCUPATION
Costumed Adventurer

BASE Suicide Slum, Metropolis

HEIGHT 5 ft 7 in WEIGHT 130 lb

EYES Blue HAIR Black

FIRST APPEARANCE
THE ADVENTURES OF
SUPERMAN #500
(June 1993)

LATEST GEAR
Superboy's costume reflects his own personal style and drive towards independence. The shades are just a stylish accessory.

Roxy

Officer-in-training Roxy Leech is the daughter of Rex Leech, an underhanded entrepreneur who once tried to capitalize on Superboy's fame. Roxy's crush on Superboy led to a lasting friendship and to her donation of genetic material to save the teen clone from fatal cellular degeneration.

TANA MOON

Superboy's first great love was Tana Moon, a Metropolis reporter who found romance with the teen hero in Hawaii, her ancestral home. During Superboy's battle with an evil cloning consortium known as "The Agenda," Tana was killed when the vengeful Amanda Spence electrocuted her. Tana's death marked the end of innocence for Superboy.

AMANDA STRIKES AGAIN
As leader of The Agenda, Amanda Spence schemed to destroy Superboy, blaming the Kid for the death of her father, Cadmus Director Paul Westfield. Since murdering Tana Moon, Amanda has altered her genetic makeup and is able to morph her now-inhuman body into a variety of deadly weapons!

51

"THEN SUPERMAN CAME ZOOMING OUT OF THE SKY, LIKE A MISSILE..."

"...NO, LIKE A GUARDIAN ANGEL..."

"HE NOT ONLY SAVED MY LIFE...HE CHANGED IT..."

STEEL

JOHN HENRY IRONS is a hero forged from the same mold as Superman. When the Man of Tomorrow saved Irons from a fatal fall off a Metropolis skyscraper, he challenged the construction worker to make his life count for something. A former weapons engineer for the ruthless AmerTek company, Irons longed to atone for the deaths his designs caused. After the Man of Tomorrow died in battle with Doomsday, Irons got his chance. He soared over Metropolis in high-tech armor, smashing crime with a sledgehammer to honor the memory of Superman, his savior!

Steel wears one of Superman's crimson cloaks, a gift from the Man of Tomorrow

FALLING DOWN

After quitting AmerTek, Irons went into hiding to avoid permanent termination. He worked the "high steel" atop building girders until Superman changed his life.

WEAPONS DESTROYER

As Steel, John Henry Irons crusaded to dismantle AmerTek's weapons programs, including the destruction of every last BG-60, the deadly assault rifle he had designed, nicknamed "The Toastmaster."

Inertial dampeners within hammer increase its striking power

TEMPERED STEEL

Originally, Steel mimicked Superman's abilities with feats of engineering. He built a bulletproof suit of armor, with computerized pneumatic exoskeletal joints that enhanced his own strength to superhuman levels. Boot jets enabled him to fly like the *other* Man of Steel. His great hammer provided him with a power-punch befitting a stand-in Superman.

PARTNERS IN CRIME-FIGHTING

Superman is proud to call John Henry Irons his partner. Irons helped the Man of Steel rebuild his Fortress of Solitude, which is now computer-linked to Irons's SteelWorks headquarters, an abandoned arms factory in Suicide Slum.

NATASHA

Steel's niece, Natasha Jasmine Irons, lives with him at the SteelWorks while attending high school in Metropolis. She once planned to become a doctor, but currently works as her uncle's lab assistant, displaying a natural talent as a structural and electronic engineer. John Henry hopes that Natasha will one day follow in his scientific footsteps. Nat, meanwhile, is learning all she can about the Kryptonian technology now linked to her home.

EMPTY SUITS!
During Brainiac 13's millennial takeover of Metropolis, John Henry had to fight his own hollow armor prototypes, which had been brought to robotic life by Brainiac 13's computer virus!

Even without his Steel armor, Irons tackles a problem with ample brains, brawn … and his trusty sledgehammer!

TEAM SUPERMAN
In Superman's absence, or if the Man of Tomorrow is in need of assistance, Steel often coordinates and leads "Team Superman," a cadre of S-shield-wearing heroes including himself, Supergirl, and Superboy. Steel provided this Super-Squad with stealthy combat-garb, protecting them from the necrotic touch of Kancer as they aided Superman in battle with General Zod and the armies of Pokolistan.

THE DEATH OF STEEL

Irons suffered mortal wounds releasing Doomsday from the JLA Watchtower to battle Imperiex. Superman was unable to turn away the Black Racer, a being who gathers perished souls and ushers them into the afterlife. This time, however, the Black Racer delivered Irons to Apokolips, where the evil Darkseid restored life to Irons's body. Steel is alive, but at what cost no one knows.

REAL NAME
John Henry Irons

OCCUPATION Engineer

BASE Metropolis

HEIGHT 6 ft 7 in **WEIGHT** 210 lb

EYES Brown **HAIR** None

FIRST APPEARANCE
THE ADVENTURES OF SUPERMAN #500
(June 1993)

Darkseid placed Irons in the Entropy Aegis, a burned-out Imperiex-Probe altered by Apokoliptic science. Steel's new armor is far superior to his previous suits, but its Apokoliptic upgrades make it more of a curse than a blessing.

GUARDIANS

SUPERMAN ISN'T THE ONLY good guy in Metropolis: he has inspired other crime fighters. Gangbuster owes his secret identity to Superman; Strange Visitor's stylish suit once belonged to the Man of Steel; the Supermen of America combat teen violence; former boxer Bibbo will knuckle-dust anyone threatening his town; and Thorn fights injustice for her own reasons. The Special Crimes Unit is the city's official response to super-powered villainy.

Former heavyweight boxer Bibbo still packs a mean punch!

BIBBO BIBBOWSKI

The proprietor of the Ace O' Clubs waterfront tavern, "Bibbo" Bibbowski is a former heavyweight boxing contender and longshoreman who regards himself as a personal friend of Superman. As such, the hard-fisted hooligan vigorously defends his "fav'rit" hero. He also stands up for Metropolis, especially the downtrodden denizens of Suicide Slum.

Gangbuster's vest, gloves, and helmet are reinforced with bulletproof Kevlar. His goggles are shatterproof.

GANGBUSTER

Schoolteacher José Delgado donned the Kevlar-lined body armor and riot helmet of Gangbuster to break up the street gangs terrorizing Suicide Slum. Gangbuster possesses no metahuman abilities, although Delgado was once a Golden Gloves boxing champion. When his fists aren't enough, Gangbuster knocks some sense into criminals with a pair of nunchakus, or shocks them into submission with an electrifying taser!

Sharon Vance and Kismet merged to become Strange Visitor, who sacrificed herself to shield Superman from Imperiex.

STRANGE VISITOR

Librarian Sharon Vance grew up alongside Clark Kent in Smallville. And like Kent, Sharon journeyed to Metropolis to find her destiny. On the way there, Sharon's airplane was struck by the essence of Kismet, a "guardian of reality" who sought shelter in Sharon's body. Sharon died that day, but Kismet briefly kept her spirit alive as the electromagnetically powered Strange Visitor, clad in Superman's former containment suit.

SUPERMEN OF AMERICA

Clockwise from left: Loser, Pyrogen, Maximum, Brahma, White Lotus, Outburst.

Once sponsored by Lex Luthor but no longer in his employ, the Supermen of America were formed when the Man of Steel declared himself King of the World! Outburst (Mitch Andersen) manipulates magnetic fields; White Lotus (Nona Lin-Baker) is an unparalleled martial artist; Brahma (Cal Usjak) is super-strong and invulnerable. Pyrogen (Claudio Tielli) is pyrokinetic, controlling flames and fire; Loser (Theo Storm) possesses an impenetrable dermal shield; and Maximum (Max Williams) channels bursts of superhuman energy.

SPECIAL CRIMES UNIT

Armed to the teeth, the Metropolis Special Crimes Unit is uniquely trained to handle anything from metahuman crime sprees to marauding alien invaders. Unfortunately, both are frequent problems in a city that is home to a strange visitor from another planet. Commanded by veteran Police Inspector Dan Turpin, the S.C.U. is the first law enforcement presence on the scene when super-villains strike. And with the S.C.U. brandishing an arsenal of non-lethal deterrents and tank-like Leviathan battlesuits, the safety of Metropolis is in good hands!

SAFE WEAPONS

Designed by John Henry Irons, the S.C.U. Leviathan battlesuits are modeled after Superman's Kryptonian Warsuit. Each Leviathan – land, air, and sea mobile – utilizes encephalo-sensitive command and response. A "sonic discombobulator" gun is one of many interchangeable apparatus available in the Leviathan's arsenal of non-lethal deterrents.

S.C.U. Leviathans deploy plastimorphic "bubble guns" to quell a prison uprising on Stryker's Island.

WE HAVE A VISITOR!

THORN

Rose Forrest became a costumed champion when the city's criminal cartel known as "The 100" murdered her police detective father. At night, Rose's alter ego takes over, forcing this otherwise gentle woman to wage war on Metropolis's mobsters as the briar-hurling tigress Thorn. Rose is totally unaware of her alter ego's nocturnal adventures.

Maggie Sawyer and Dan Turpin lead well-armed S.C.U. officers into the fray.

SUPERGIRL

SHE WAS MOLDED out of protoplasm. From this most basic substance of life came a formless individual in search of identity. Born in a pocket universe where Kryptonian criminals decimated her Earth, the being known as "Matrix" found peace on Superman's adopted world. Here, she learned goodness from the Kents, the evils of deception from Lex Luthor, and the sacrifices of heroism from the Man of Steel, who inspired her to become a "Supergirl." But she lacked a true human soul until merging with the dying Linda Danvers, redeeming them both in the process.

MATRIX

A benevolent Lex Luthor from a pocket universe fabricated Matrix. He sent the shape-changing protoplasm to Earth to secure Superman's help in defeating rogue Kryptonians. Luthor perished, as did his world. Wounded, Matrix returned with Superman to his Earth to convalesce with the Kents. "Mae" then journeyed to Metropolis. There she was seduced by a Luthor not half as heroic as her creator.

With a touch, Supergirl and Linda became one being!

LINDA DANVERS

Young and rebellious, Linda Danvers flirted with disaster when she fell under the spell of the charismatic Buzz, who made her a human offering to the demonic Lord Chakat. Fortunately, Supergirl intervened and was forced to physically merge with Linda in order to save her life. The synthetic Supergirl gained a human soul in her union with Linda, becoming an Earth-born angel more powerful than her previous incarnation.

BUZZ

This demon from Hell trapped in human form fell in love with the Earth-bound angel Supergirl, a being he helped create. Buzz now guides the Maid of Might in search of the "Chaos Stream" leading to the angelic entity that was once part of her.

FIREPOWER

Supergirl's protoplasmic body allowed her to morph her features at will and assume any guise. In addition, the Maid of Might wielded telekinetic abilities, great strength, and the power of flight. In her angelic form, Supergirl possessed flame-vision and fiery wings which enabled her to fly, teleport between locations, and judge the sins of the wicked.

A NEW DIRECTION

Recently, Supergirl sacrificed her angelic spirit in order to destroy the Carnivore, an unholy embodiment of evil. What *was* the Girl of Steel is now separated from Linda Danvers, who still retains a portion of her former might. Linda now trails the "Chaos Stream" in hopes of reuniting with the spirit who once saved her life and spared her soul.

> SHOULD'VE KNOWN. SUPERMAN DIED AND ALL THE SUPERMAN WANNABES SHOWED UP. NOW IT'S *SUPERGIRL* PRETENDERS!

MAID OF MIGHT

No one was more surprised to see Supergirl alive than the Man of Steel whose shield she proudly wears. Superman believed the Maid of Might had been killed in her apocalyptic battle with the Carnivore. Happily, he later found her alive and well … and tearing up downtown Metropolis while battling the Prankster, who was wearing Steel's high-tech armor.

SUPER-MAKEOVER

Linda tested her remaining powers against the super-villain Riot, cobbling together a makeshift uniform in a Metropolis shop besieged by the multiplying menace. The Girl of Steel now wears a miniskirt, T-shirt, short cape, and lace-up boots, with a blonde wig concealing her secret identity. Linda possesses some of Supergirl's formidable strength, but not her ability to fly. She can, however, leap approximately one-eighth of a mile.

REAL NAME Linda Danvers

OCCUPATION Artist

BASE Leesville

HEIGHT 5 ft 5 in **WEIGHT** 125 lb

EYES Blue **HAIR** Brown

FIRST APPEARANCE
SUPERMAN #16
(April 1988)

HER WORLD AT WAR

While Linda continues to search for the original Supergirl's spirit, she still retains some of her memories. Thus, the world-razing Imperiex's attack on Kansas struck a raw nerve in the Maid of Might, who once lived with the Kents in Smallville. Though unable to find her missing surrogate parents during the conflict, Supergirl returned to Linda Danvers's home in Leesburg to successfully thwart one of Imperiex's destructive probes.

A NEW SUPERGIRL

LAST SON OF KRYPTON no more! Superman thought he was alone in the universe, sole survivor of a dead planet. That is, until cousin Kara Zor-El arrived on Earth from the Man of Steel's homeworld. But Kara's relationship to Kal-El of Krypton was more than coincidental, and the fact that now *two* superpowered Kryptonians would be calling Earth their home was a cause for concern!

SPLASHDOWN
Kara's spacecraft had been entombed in Kryptonian rock after the planet exploded. Kept alive in suspended animation, the kryptonite asteroid containing Kara's ship found its way to Earth, trailing Kal-El's navigational signal. It eventually fell to Earth amid a meteor shower over Gotham Bay, where it was discovered by Batman!

NEW IN TOWN
Meanwhile Kara swam to the surface and stole away in the Batboat. Naked, speaking only Kryptonese, she fended off leering longshoremen and obtained a coat. An Earth vehicle bounced off her body in a crunch of twisted metal and Kara looked on, wide-eyed. Then a changing traffic light surprised her; Kara treated this perceived threat with a blast of heat vision!

AMONG THE AMAZONS
Kara's powers continued to develop under the rays of Earth's yellow sun. Superman welcomed his cousin, but Batman was ill at ease; he disliked knowing so little about Kara and her origins. Unknown to Superman, the Dark Knight convinced Wonder Woman to take custody of Kara and give her refuge on the island of Themyscira, where the Amazon sisterhood would school Superman's cousin in the ways of both war and peace.

APOKOLIPS NOW!

Unfortunately, Darkseid was only too aware of Kara's existence! He dispatched his Female Furies to kidnap Kara. Superman, Batman, Wonder Woman, and the Amazons fought valiantly, but Kara disappeared in a Boom Tube to Apokolips. Kara's good friend, the heroine Harbinger, died trying to prevent Kara's abduction.

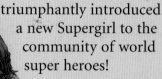

REAL NAME Kara Zor-El

OCCUPATION Adventurer

BASE Metropolis

HEIGHT 5 ft 5 in **WEIGHT** 135 lb

EYES Blue **HAIR** Blonde

FIRST APPEARANCE
ACTION COMICS #252
(May 1959)

THE END OF SUPERGIRL?

Journeying to Apokolips, the heroes found Kara in Darkseid's thrall! Batman, Wonder Woman, and their ally Big Barda engaged the Female Furies and Warhounds of Apokolips as Superman battled Darkseid for Kara's soul. Risking his own life, the Man of Steel wore a kryptonite ring to break Darkseid's grip on Kara, and they all returned to Earth. When Darkseid pursued Kara, Superman faked his cousin's death and defeated the villain. Later, he triumphantly introduced a new Supergirl to the community of world super heroes!

BATMAN'S CONCERN
Inscribed on Kara's spacecraft was the legend: "This vessel carries my daughter, Kara Zor-El from the now dead planet Krypton. Treat her as you would your own child for you will see the treasure she will be for your world." The Dark Knight worried that this "treasure" might spell "trouble" or "terror"!

SECRETS OF THE MAN OF STEEL

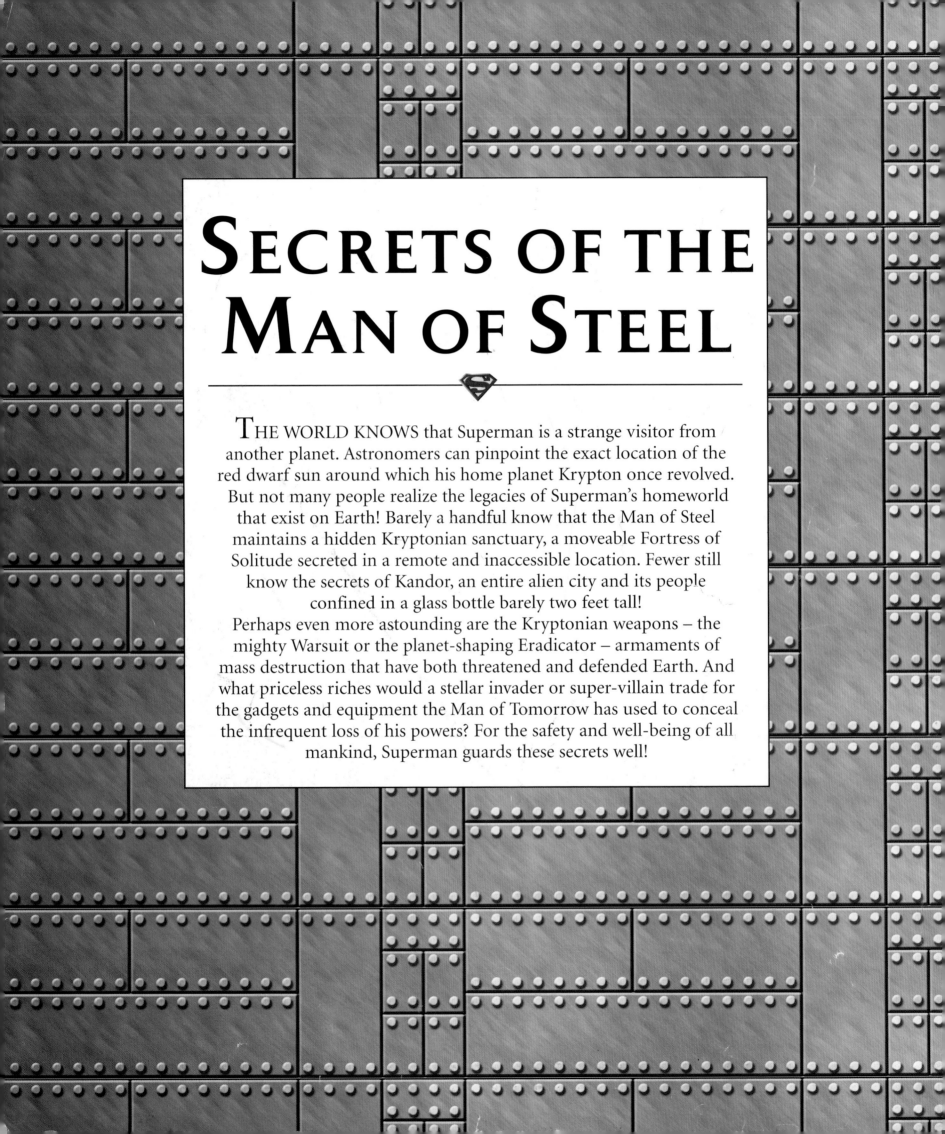

THE WORLD KNOWS that Superman is a strange visitor from another planet. Astronomers can pinpoint the exact location of the red dwarf sun around which his home planet Krypton once revolved. But not many people realize the legacies of Superman's homeworld that exist on Earth! Barely a handful know that the Man of Steel maintains a hidden Kryptonian sanctuary, a moveable Fortress of Solitude secreted in a remote and inaccessible location. Fewer still know the secrets of Kandor, an entire alien city and its people confined in a glass bottle barely two feet tall!

Perhaps even more astounding are the Kryptonian weapons – the mighty Warsuit or the planet-shaping Eradicator – armaments of mass destruction that have both threatened and defended Earth. And what priceless riches would a stellar invader or super-villain trade for the gadgets and equipment the Man of Tomorrow has used to conceal the infrequent loss of his powers? For the safety and well-being of all mankind, Superman guards these secrets well!

THE FORTRESS

SUPERMAN'S SECRET SANCTUARY is bigger than it appears, yet the Man of Steel can balance the containment sphere housing his "Fortress of Solitude" on the tip of one finger. Originally conceived as a safe repository for preserving Kryptonian culture and artifacts, Superman utilizes the Fortress – now housed inside an infinite interdimensional space – as an occasional escape from the demands of heroism. Hidden high atop a mountain ice ledge, the Fortress remains safe and secure, accessible only to the Last Son of Krypton and his closest allies!

REMOTE ACCESS
Since the fixed location of his previous Antarctic Fortress made it an easy target, Superman appreciates his now mobile refuge. Only Superman is strong enough to align the sphere's complex puzzle-plates.

FAITHFUL SERVANT
Primary maintenance of the Fortress is carried out by Kelex, a duplicate of Jor-El's robotic servant on Krypton. Like Superman's original sanctuary, Kelex was reconstructed according to Kryptonian specifications by the Eradicator device. Kelex is utterly loyal to Superman and tirelessly services the Fortress. Kelex had been polite and precise in all utterances, but Natasha Irons altered his response circuitry to make the robot more user-friendly. Kelex now spices its speech with street slang and refers to the Man of Steel as "Big Blue."

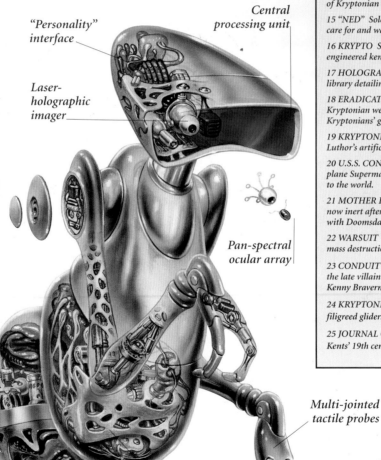

"Personality" interface

Central processing unit

Laser-holographic imager

Pan-spectral ocular array

Techno-organic memory cluster

Multi-jointed tactile probes

Advanced alloy endoskeleton

INTO THE SPHERE
John Henry Irons conceived the technology enabling Superman to build his Fortress within a dimension of unlimited space known as a tesseract.

Natasha watches Superman enter the Fortress sphere for the first time.

1 **KRYPTONIAN POWER CRYSTALS** *These giant gems power the Fortress via safe, self-sustaining, and waste-free cold fusion.*

2 **TESSERACT SPHERE** *Facsimile of the larger orb allowing Superman access to the tesseract enclosing the Fortress.*

3 **KRYPTON MEMORIAL** *Twin holographic depictions of Jor-El and Lara remind Superman of his home planet.*

4 **BIRTH MATRIX** *Replica of the artificial womb and star-drive which carried Superman to Earth.*

5 **PHANTOM ZONE PORTAL** *A Soliton-Generator provides a stable doorway into the extra-dimensional Zone.*

6 **PHANTOM ZONE CONTROL** *Automated systems monitor energy surges and all movement in and out of the Zone.*

7 **KELEX** *Robot in charge of maintenance and protection.*

8 **KANDOR** *Dimensionally challenged "Bottle City" and its plethora of alien citizens caught in trans-spatial flux.*

9 **CONTROL HUB** *Monitor banks enable Superman to maintain vigil over the Earth.*

10 **SPECNAP** *John Henry Irons's Spectral Nexus Apparatus maintains the tesseract surrounding the Fortress of Solitude.*

11 **KRYPTONOPOLIS** *Crystalline diorama of the once great Kryptonian capital city.*

12 **SLAG POOL** *Molten bath used by Superman to cleanse his person and costume of extra-terrestrial microorganisms.*

13 **CENTRAL COMPUTER NEXUS** *Links Fortress automated systems and provides power boosts to any area or mechanism in mere nanoseconds.*

14 **SERVICE ROBOT** *Irons's updated designs feature a hybridization of Kryptonian and Earthly technologies.*

15 **"NED"** *Sole remaining Superman-Robot whose prime directive is to care for and watch over Krypto.*

16 **KRYPTO** *Superman's dog now lives in a specially engineered kennel inside the Fortress.*

17 **HOLOGRAPHIC ARCHIVE** *Encyclopedic holo-library detailing Superman's life and exploits.*

18 **ERADICATOR** *Spent casing of the Kryptonian weapon designed to ensure Kryptonians' genetic purity.*

19 **KRYPTONITE** *Radiation-depleted sample of Lex Luthor's artificially synthesized kryptonite.*

20 **U.S.S. CONSTITUTION** *Miniature replica of the crashing space-plane Superman once saved from destruction, thus revealing himself to the world.*

21 **MOTHER BOX** *One of the New Gods' sentient super-computers, now inert after expending her energies aiding Superman in battle with Doomsday.*

22 **WARSUIT** *Fully armed and operational Kryptonian weapon of mass destruction.*

23 **CONDUIT'S COILS** *The kryptonite-fueled cables wielded by the late villain Conduit, a.k.a. Clark Kent's childhood friend Kenny Braverman.*

24 **KRYPTONIAN SKYSHIP** *Scale model of the swift and light filigreed gliders of ancient Krypton.*

25 **JOURNAL OF SILAS KENT** *Personal account of the ancestral Kents' 19th century migration to the frontier Kansas Territory.*

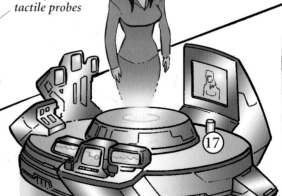

Superman's favorite holographic image

For Tomorrow

WHAT IF A CATASTROPHE HIT EARTH similar to the one that destroyed Krypton? This was Lois Lane's question to her husband. Krypton's Last Son had no answer. But the dilemma tugged at his mind, Superman's father, Jor-El, had created the interdimensional Phantom Zone as a prison for Krypton's worst criminals. Superman resolved to remake the Zone using Kryptonian technology into a utopian refuge for Earth's population should the planet ever suffer the same fate as Krypton. But something went badly wrong with Superman's dream…

FATHER DANIEL
A million people had mysteriously vanished across the globe… and Lois was one of them! Shaken to the core, Superman confided in Father Daniel Leone, a Catholic priest whose own faith was being tested by a deadly cancer.

GENERAL NOX
Superman traced the source of the vanishings to a war-torn country half a world away. The only way Superman could end the war was by allowing "freedom-fighter" General Nox to take power. Unfortunately, Nox was left in control of the mysterious weapon responsible for the vanishings.

ELEMENTAL FORCES
Nox's men mercilessly gunned down any opposition. From the sand where their enemies' bodies lay, the enigmatic witch known as Halcyon invoked the elemental spirits of the Earth—titanic creatures composed of Rock, Air, Fire, and Water—to rise up and battle the "foreigner" Superman. Fortunately, the Man of Steel convinced these monsters of the utter futility of their actions, and the Elementals gave up and disappeared back into the earth.

EQUUS
Equus was a bionic one-man army with crocodilian skin employed by General Nox. Despite his steroid-fueled strength, Equus was no match for Superman, so he took Nox hostage and activated the vanishing weapon. In a flash, both man and machine-man disappeared, as did 300,000 more innocent individuals all over the world. Superman's desperation grew.

UTOPIA

Wonder Woman saved Leone and another interloper, the mercenary Mr. Orr, before the Fortress imploded. Superman vanished by activating the weapon, a Phantom Zone Projector, and found himself in a paradise of his own making, Metropia. There he found Lois Lane and all the other vanished people!

AUTO-DESTRUCT

Accompanied by Father Leone, Superman took the vanishing weapon back to his Fortress of Solitude. Just as he had finally figured out the weapon's secret, Wonder Woman breached the Fortress's walls, and Superman's arctic refuge self-destructed!

THAT'S A VERY *MERCENARY* WAY TO GO THROUGH LIFE.

YEAH, WELL...

EQUUS IV

Mister Orr promised Father Leone a cure for cancer. What Orr didn't tell the stricken priest was that his employers had merely improved upon cancer, harnessing the rogue mutagenic cells to turn Leone into the latest One Man Army Corps, Equus IV!

EQUUS TIMES TWO

Many people, including Lois Lane, believed in Superman's paradise. Others wanted to destroy it, including the vanished Equus III. He seized the Phantom Zone Projector, but then fell afoul of Equus IV. The two cyborgs tumbled into a dimensional rift as Metropia dissolved!

BROTHER!

NOOOOO...

ZOD'S LAW

When Superman created Metropia, he assumed the Phantom Zone was devoid of life. However, the Zone's most dangerous prisoner—put there by Jor-El himself—remained. Zod destroyed Metropia with his army and although Superman battled him to a standstill, his fate remains a mystery.

A NEW FORTRESS

In the end, the Man of Steel chose to rebuild his Fortress of Solitude deep within the rain forests of South America. He decided to surround himself with life, instead of isolating himself amid bleak, arctic ice.

KANDOR

THE BOTTLE CITY Kandor is home to thousands of beings believed to have been abducted by the alien wizard Tolos and imprisoned between dimensional planes. Superman succeeded in liberating the Kandorians from Tolos, safeguarding their shrunken world inside his original Fortress of Solitude. But when a kryptonite warhead decimated Superman's secret sanctuary, desperate Kandorian scientists had no choice but to cast their bottle city adrift in the Phantom Zone! Superman has since collected the city and placed it in a bottle containment once more. There Kandor remains until it can one day be freed from its trans-dimensional prison.

CITY IN A BOTTLE

Superman explored the remains of Kandor while visiting an alternate Krypton before its destruction. Instead of finding the ruins of the once great capital razed by Black Zero's nuclear device, the Man of Steel learned that Kandor – prior to its trans-dimensional disappearance – was a vast internment camp for aliens.

SOCIAL UNREST

Kandor is a miniaturized metropolis teeming with many diverse and sometimes discordant alien cultures. As a result, the bottle city has long struggled with civil strife. Species differences once divided ghettoized sections of Kandor, where countless generations have subsisted by growing and synthesizing just enough food to survive their continued imprisonment under Tolos.

Superman later reconstructed Tolos' laboratory bottle to keep Kandor stable and secure in his Fortress of Solitude.

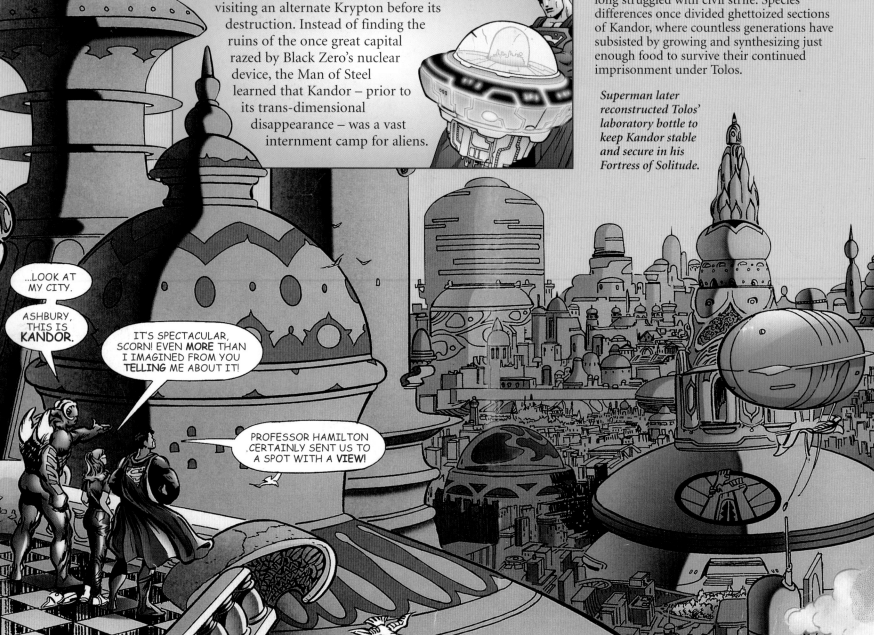

SCORN

The mighty Ceritak is the son of gentle Cerimul, a late Elder of Kandor's ruling Council. While Cerimul struggled to unite Kandor in peace following its liberation from Tolos, Ceritak escaped the bottle city and fled to Metropolis. His misunderstood attempts to overcome the language barrier earned the horned Kandorian the nickname "Scorn" from the Metropolitan media chronicling his exploits.

Scorn abdicated a Kandorian Council seat to his sister Cerizah, preferring freedom in Metropolis to leadership in Kandor.

ASHBURY!

PLEASE... BE CAREFUL!

ASHBURY ARMSTRONG

Daughter of *Daily Planet* columnist Dirk Armstrong, blind Ashbury Armstrong was Scorn's first friend in Metropolis. While visiting Scorn's native Kandor, Ashbury received Kandorian goggles that restored her sight. "Beauty" to his "Beast," she and Scorn have returned to Earth, where they remain devoted companions.

THE PHANTOM ZONE

The interdimensional space known to Superman as the "Phantom Zone" was discovered by his own Kryptonian ancestor Kem-L centuries ago. Also known as the "Ghost Zone," this ethereal emptiness served as a cosmic catchall for Krypton's detritus. Menacing life forms – the result of Kryptonians' dangerous genetic tinkering – were expelled into the Phantom Zone along with hazardous mechanisms and possibly even Krypton's criminal malcontents, exiled for eternity in the endless void!

PARTICLE BEAM SET!

TELEMETRIES SET!

OPEN LOCK 1, LOCK 2, LOCK 3!

Superman's physical form is twisted like taffy as he leaves the "solid" universe for the Phantom Zone.

The Man of Steel enters the void via the Soliton-Generator, a "Phantom Zone Projector" first designed by Kem-L.

Inside the Phantom Zone, Superman encounters the maddened manifestation of Kem-L.

GODFALL

TO THE DENIZENS OF KANDOR, what is Superman if not a god? After all, the Man of Steel safeguarded the bottle city in his Fortress of Solitude and provided for its every need. Fighting for his life against Brainiac thousands of years in the future, Superman was hurled back through time. To make his way home, the Last Son of Krypton focused on his emotional bonds to loved ones to free himself from the timestream. But instead of emerging on Earth and in Metropolis, Superman found himself on alien soil. Quite literally, this god was pulled down from heaven and into a Kandor much changed from the bottle city Superman once knew.

CITY IN A BOTTLE
An alien city shrunken and stolen by Brainiac, Kandor was rescued by Superman. Kept in his fortress, Kandor fell victim to spatial temporal disjunction. In a year, the city aged a century, turning into a hate-divided society based on a Superman cult.

TROUBLED MAN

When he awoke in Kandor, Superman was Kal-El in a city that believed itself the last bastion of Kryptonian civilization; his parents Jor-El and Lara were alive; Kal had a mundane job and was married to the lovely Lyla. Yet Kal had dreams larger than tiny Kandor.

ALIEN UNREST

Despite maintaining the technological and cultural glory that was once Krypton, Kandor was a city at odds with itself. Civil strife threatened the city. The humanoid populace of the original Kandor enjoyed much greater freedoms than the minority alien population. A gang of alien guerilla bikers led by the charismatic Basqat led the fight for equal rights for all, a rebellion soon targeting Undersecretary of the Kryptonian Council Kal-El and his alien wife, Lyla!

SUCK GLASS, FASCIST PRETTY-BOY!

AIIEEEEE!

LYLA!

LEAVE ME ALONE--!!!

FATAL ERROR

Kal had no memory that he was
Superman. But when attacked by Basqat's
gang, Kal fought back like a true Man of
Steel. He had super strength. He flew. His
eyes emitted heat beams. Unfortunately,
he also had freezing breath that froze his
neighbor Kon and Kon's parents to
death… or so he *thought*.

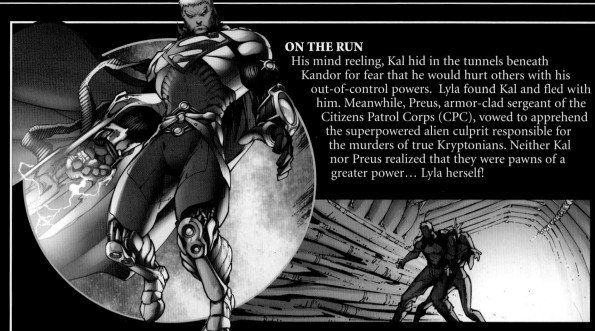

ON THE RUN

His mind reeling, Kal hid in the tunnels beneath
Kandor for fear that he would hurt others with his
out-of-control powers. Lyla found Kal and fled with
him. Meanwhile, Preus, armor-clad sergeant of the
Citizens Patrol Corps (CPC), vowed to apprehend
the superpowered alien culprit responsible for
the murders of true Kryptonians. Neither Kal
nor Preus realized that they were pawns of a
greater power… Lyla herself!

TAKEN OVER

With Preus in pursuit, Lyla revealed the truth to Kal: she was
an alien "empireth" whose every cell was telepathic. During
Kandor's century of strife, Lyla had lost faith in the city's *de
facto* god, Superman. And so she plotted to pull him down
into the bottle city to force him to experience Kandor's
suffering. Lyla constructed false memories—including the
deaths of Kon and his parents—to humble the once-mighty
Man of Steel. She later took over Superman's powers and set
out to become a goddesss in present-day Metropolis!

AWAKE,
KANDOR
A GODDESS IS
BORN!

LYLA?

LYLA DEPARTS

Lyla disappeared in a
nova-bright explosion that
seemingly consumed Preus.
However Preus lived, his
armor bonded to his flesh
and his mind consumed
with hatred for Superman.

PREUS ATTACKS!

Superman freed himself from
Kandor, and Basqat's alien gang
came along for the ride to help
him put a stop to Lyla's delusions.
Unfortunately, alien-hunter Preus
also arrived in Metropolis! Caught
between Preus and Lyla, each
determined to destroy the other,
Superman battled to save his city!

AAAAHHH!

THE ARMOR
COMPENSATES,
IT'S STAVED OFF
THE "EXPOSURE
SICKNESS"…

…AND IT'S
BUILT TO TURN
THE MALICE OF YOUR
DEGENERATE
MIND BACK
UPON YOU!

GOODBYE,
KAL-EL

SUPER-TECH

SOMETIMES SUPERPOWERS fail when a Man of Steel needs them most. There are even occasions when Superman must rely upon special equipment to fight the good fight. Whether donning a Warsuit, or an oxygen mask to fly through space, the Man of Tomorrow chooses discretion over a blind faith in his abilities. Frequently, Superman calls upon the scientific expertise of S.T.A.R. Labs, John Henry Irons or Professor Emil Hamilton to provide him with the technological edge to keep the world safe!

BATTLE-TECH

A Warsuit pilot floats semi-conscious in a nutrient-rich fluid within the behemoth's chest cavity. Linked telepathically to a techno-organic brain, he relies on bio-probe synaptic tendrils to drive the Warsuit as if it were an extension of his own body.

ROBOT FIGHTERS

When Dominus destroyed Superman's Fortress of Solitude by using LexCorp Tower as a kryptonite missile, the Man of Steel sought refuge inside his Kryptonian Warsuit from the lingering radiation. So Dominus used his reality-altering powers to create his own telekinetic behemoth and shatter Kal-El's armor!

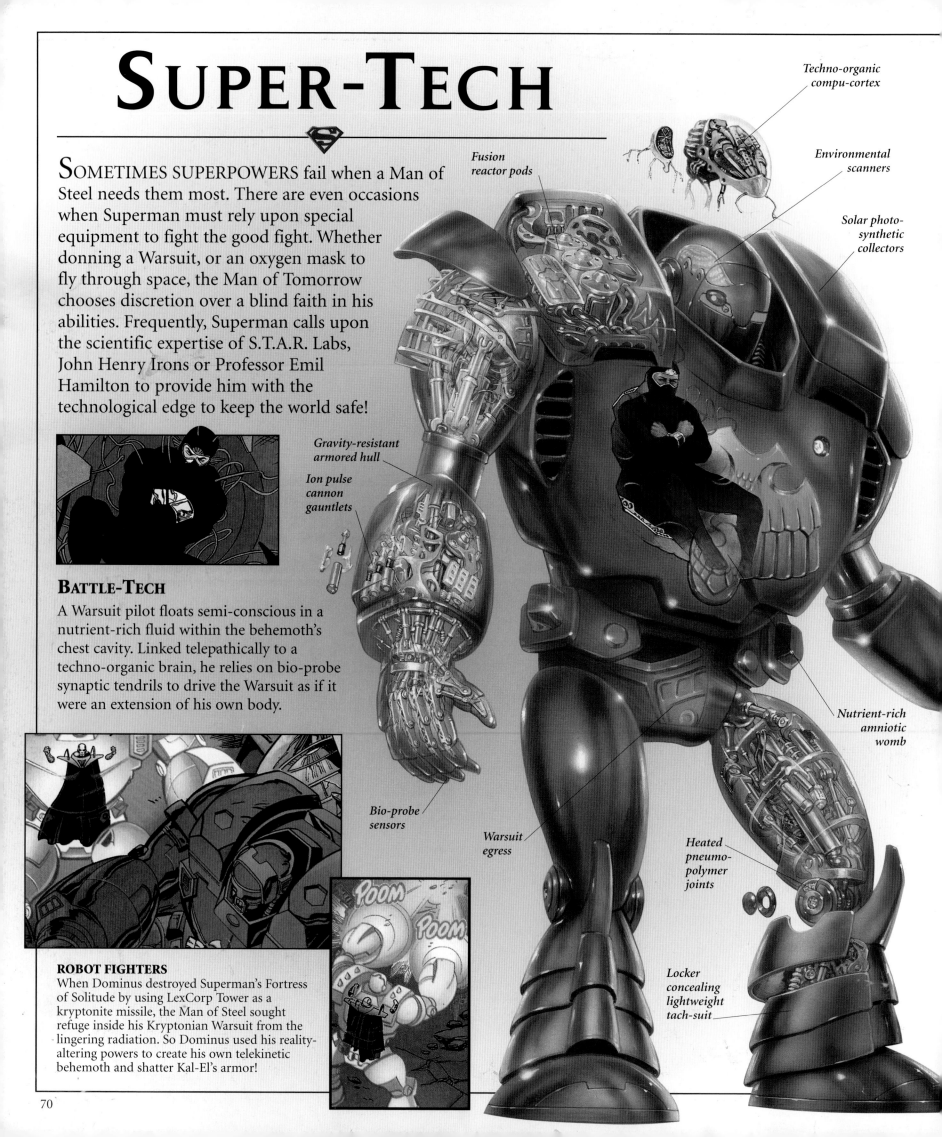

Techno-organic compu-cortex

Environmental scanners

Solar photo-synthetic collectors

Fusion reactor pods

Gravity-resistant armored hull

Ion pulse cannon gauntlets

Nutrient-rich amniotic womb

Bio-probe sensors

Warsuit egress

Heated pneumo-polymer joints

Locker concealing lightweight tach-suit

POOM

POOM

MOTHER BOX

This highly advanced and sentient computer is able to summon space-warping Boom Tubes, heal injuries, and even outfit Superman's costume for battle with its signature PING! Superman borrowed it from the New Gods to battle Doomsday on distant Apokolips. The Mother Box transported him there in the blink of an eye!

IRON-MAKER

In civilian guise, John Henry Irons (a.k.a. Steel) uses his engineering savvy to aid Superman. With Professor Emil Hamilton, Irons constructed a "Phantom Zone Projector." The device allowed the Man of Steel to glimpse Krypton's past by translating the information encoded on a Kryptonian isobar crystal directly into Superman's mind.

Superman beheld many wondrous sights as he viewed the living Krypton through the ocular-array of the Phantom Zone Projector!

Irons designed this aquanaut suit for deep-sea volcanic vent exploration, but then miniaturized the armor to take a fantastic voyage within Superman's kryptonite-poisoned body!

SUPERMAN'S OXYGEN MASK

When Superman exiled himself from Earth, he traveled across deep space using a breathing apparatus and experimental teleportation harness. Invented by Professor Hamilton, the oxygen unit could be recharged in breathable atmospheres. The teleportation device, provided by Vegan star system freedom fighters the Omega Men, allowed for short jumps across the interstellar void. However, it required careful calibration for exact destinations, often leaving the Man of Steel lost in space.

Microwave transmitter vox in "smart-polymer" mask

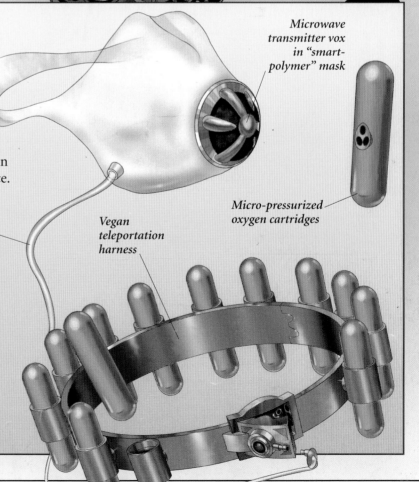

Self-sealing circulatory tube

Vegan teleportation harness

Micro-pressurized oxygen cartridges

MISSION TO MARS

Professor Hamilton's oxygen apparatus aided the Man of Tomorrow on his special sojourn to Mars, where he repaired a stranded NASA exploratory rover. Superman replaced a faulty battery pack on the lander, enabling it to continue surveying the red planet's surface.

THE ERADICATCR

THE SOUL OF KRYPTON resides in the Eradicator. Built by Superman's ancestor Kem-L, the Eradicator was devised as a weapon to alter the genetics of Kryptonians and bind them to their planet. Millennia later, the Eradicator gained a will of its own and determined to restore Krypton's heritage. It possessed the Man of Steel, built his first Fortress of Solitude, and tried to remake Earth into a new Krypton. When the Man of Steel died battling Doomsday, the Eradicator served as a replacement Superman. It later joined with the soul of an Earthman before evolving yet again.

The Eradicator's powers included flight, super-strength, heat vision, and the ability to emit pulsing energy blasts from his fists!

KRYPTON'S SAVIOR

After the Man of Steel's fatal clash with Doomsday, the Eradicator placed the hero's body in a Kryptonian rejuvenation chamber, created a human shell for itself, and assumed Superman's guise. When Superman awoke to battle the alliance of Cyborg and Mongul, the Eradicator protected the Last Son of Krypton yet again by shielding him from a kryptonite pulse that would have killed him – *permanently*!

DR. DAVID CONNOR

After the Cyborg's defeat, the Eradicator's shell bonded with S.T.A.R. Labs' Dr. David Connor, who was dying of cancer. Connor, now a Kryptonian/human hybrid, vainly struggled to control the Eradicator's annihilation program, which caused the death of his wife and the abandonment of his children.

Bonding with the Eradicator cost David Connor his humanity.

THE WILL OF KRYPTON

When Superman's Fortress of Solitude was destroyed by Dominus, Lois Lane salvaged a Kryptonian figurine and took it back to Metropolis. The figurine activated the Eradicator program, which began renovating Lois and Clark's apartment according to Kryptonian designs. It even forced the Man of Steel into a mental duel with an illusory manifestation of his ancestor, Kem-L!

FORTRESS ERADICATOR

To his horror, David Connor realized that the Eradicator had somehow split in two. One part inhabited his hybrid body, while the primary program lay in the ruins of Superman's obliterated Fortress. When the primary program fused the ashes of the Fortress into a mountainous Kryptonian Warsuit, Connor allowed his half to be absorbed into the primary Eradicator. As the Eradicator programming wrestled with Connor's human soul for control of the Warsuit, Connor blasted the behemoth off into deep space, promising never to return to Earth.

REAL NAME
Dr. David Connor

OCCUPATION Preserver of Kryptonian Heritage

BASE Mobile

HEIGHT 6 ft 3 in **WEIGHT** 225 lb

EYES Red **HAIR** Gray

FIRST APPEARANCE
ACTION COMICS #693
(November 1993)

THE MESSAGE
But the Eradicator did return, traversing incalculable light-years to warn Superman of Earth's impending destruction by Imperiex. During its sojourn in the interstellar void, David Connor's consciousness had suffered a collapse, creating a fanatical messianic Eradicator urging Earth's doomed souls to repent their sins!

SUSPENDED ANNIHILATION
Momentarily stunning the crazed Eradicator, Superman realized that David Connor's salvation lay in devising a way to extricate him from the Kryptonian annihilator program. Meanwhile, Connor's Eradicator body was immobilized in an absolute zero staging chamber inside John Henry Irons's SteelWorks.

JOKERIZED
Unfortunately, the Eradicator was liberated from his prison by rampaging super-villains infected with the Joker's unique brand of lunacy. The Eradicator itself was "Jokerized," making the annihilator program dominant once more and forcing Superman to trap it within the null chamber of his Fortress of Solitude.

73

SUPERVILLANY

FROM ADVERSARY TO ZOD, Superman's Rogues Gallery is filled to overflowing with megalomaniacs, monsters, and Most Wanted villains from throughout the universe. Each one of them would like nothing better than to destroy the Man of Steel. The Metropolis mogul Lex Luthor would argue that the line begins and ends with him. The killing machine Doomsday would slay every last foe fool enough to get between him and the Last Son of Krypton. And for the sheer fun of it, the ever-mischievous Mr. Mxyzptlk would bring them all back to life just to torment his Super-Nemesis. Some, like Riot or Encantadora, are motivated by money. Others, like the aliens Brainiac and Darkseid, want the world … or as many worlds as they can conquer. Still more, like Bizarro or Atomic Skull, are merely misguided … but no less dangerous in their metahuman mayhem.

Only Superman can stop them all. And as long as evil threatens innocent life in Metropolis, on Earth, or beyond, the Man of Tomorrow fights a never-ending battle against impossible odds!

LEX LUTHOR

NO MAN ON EARTH is more dangerous than Lex Luthor. From the poverty of Metropolis's Suicide Slum, Luthor climbed to wealth and greatness, surveying his business empire atop the city's tallest building. And then came Superman. No longer the most powerful man in Metropolis, Luthor vowed to regain his lofty perch, even if it meant destroying the Man of Steel! A hero to few and villain to many, Luthor craves only power. And he now wields a great deal of it as President of the United States!

A BAD START

As a boy of less than humble beginnings, Lex Luthor was a close friend of young Perry White, who often witnessed the frequent domestic skirmishes between Lex's alcoholic and abusive parents. They later died in a mysterious automobile accident, the cause of which was never fully understood. The end result, however, was Lex inheriting a $300,000 insurance premium. Soon, Lex would invest the sum, escaping Suicide Slum and planting the seeds of LexCorp.

REVENGE

After his parents' deaths, Lex was sent to live with Casey and Elaine Griggs, uncaring foster parents who plotted to steal Lex's money. When fellow foster child Lena – Lex's first love – refused to aid the Griggs' scam, Casey Griggs killed her. Years later, Luthor hired Griggs to assassinate Mayor Berkowitz. The Metropolis Mogul then avenged Lena's murder by paying his hitman with a single bullet.

LENA LUTHOR

Sole heir to Lex Luthor's empire, Lena Luthor is the daughter of Lex and the Contessa Erica Alexandra del Portenza. As an infant, Lena's body was taken over by Brainiac 2.5 and later bartered away to the futuristic Brainiac 13 by Luthor himself, who sacrificed his red-haired daughter for control of Metropolis's millennial technological upgrades. Though aged to young maturity for a time, Lena is once more a normal infant in Luthor's care.

Brainiac 13 evolved Lena into a troublesome teen, who clashed with her despotic dad!

THE CONTESSA

The latest ex-wife of Lex Luthor, the Contessa Erica Alexandra del Portenza is remarkably long-lived – despite her former spouse's best intentions! President Luthor ordered a cruise missile attack upon her Siberian stronghold; however, the sultry, scheming Contessa has cheated death before ...

EMPLOYMENT TERMINATED!

Wilkins made a fatal miscalculation when he attempted to steal LexCorp's developmental teleport technology. Despite the relativity engineer's ten years of loyal employment, Luthor opted to forego a severance package and offer Wilkins a one-way trip in the untested teleporter.

ASSASSINATION ATTEMPT

Jenny Hubbard hated Lex Luthor. Years earlier, Luthor offered the truck stop waitress one million dollars to live a life of luxury with him for just one month. Hubbard refused. Haunted into delusions by her decision, Hubbard attempted to assassinate Luthor during his presidential bid. Ironically, Hubbard's act only helped to improve Luthor's public image.

HAIL TO THE CHIEF

After his revitalization of both Metropolis and Gotham City, Luthor won the U.S. Presidency with votes to spare. And while his hate for the Man of Tomorrow remains boundless, President Luthor realizes the value of diplomacy, displaying unity between himself and Superman. Luthor has shown himself to be a capable statesman, and scored high approval ratings for his leadership during the terrible Imperiex War.

REAL NAME Lex Luthor
OCCUPATION U.S. President
BASE Washington, D.C.
HEIGHT 6 ft 2 in WEIGHT 210 lb
EYES Green HAIR None
FIRST APPEARANCE
ACTION COMICS #23
(April 1940)

LexCorp

THE ENTREPRENEURIAL EMPIRE of Lex Luthor, LexCorp first soared with the development of the vanguard *Lex Wing* aircraft. LexCorp is now Metropolis's most powerful multinational conglomerate. Publicly, the company employs two thirds of the city workforce in businesses ranging from communications (LexCom) to petrochemicals (LexOil), with controlling patents on all futuristic Brainiac 13 technology. Privately, Luthor's companies engage in weapons manufacture and secret scientific research to further the mogul's unrelenting quest to eliminate Superman!

Luthor's Sea-Tracker was sabotaged by rival businessman Mr. Krisma, who plotted to publicly discredit the Metropolis mogul and nearly drowned him!

THE SEA-TRACKER

LexCorp's most anticipated new project, the *Sea-Tracker*, proved to be a billion-dollar boondoggle for the company. At its public unveiling, the automated undersea oil seeker went berserk and threatened the lives of hundreds of onlookers!

MERCY AND HOPE

Lex Luthor's gorgeous "Girls Friday," Mercy and Hope, serve double-duty now that their employer holds the highest office in the land. While not official secret service agents, President Luthor's two bodyguards are his primary security personnel in the Oval Office. They also undertake covert missions known only to President Luthor, and keep watch over the more secret underpinnings of his LexCorp financial empire. Mercy and Hope are utterly loyal to Luthor and would defend him to their dying breaths.

FEMMES FATALES

LexCorp's Human Resources department will neither confirm nor deny that Mercy and Hope are of Amazonian descent, which might explain why their martial arts skills even stagger Superman! Luthor himself often spars with his muscled minders, signaling that he's had enough of their pummeling by speaking the code word "Waterloo."

TALIA

While Luthor is U.S. President, the lovely Talia Head serves as LexCorp's interim CEO. Talia is the daughter of Rā's al Ghūl, a zealous eco-terrorist and immortal foe of Batman. Currently estranged from her father and his criminal cult, Talia has proven experience in international finance. Luthor appreciates Talia's grace under pressure and ruthlessness, traits he finds invaluable in the cutthroat world of big business.

LexAir's military-contracted Valkyrie-class attack helicopters are often used "off the books"

LexCorp Security Sentries equipped with temperature-regulated bodysuits and night-vision goggles

PRIVATE ARMY

LexCorp holdings range from banking and finance to communications and entertainment, but the company's most lucrative endeavor is arms manufacture. Selling to both the U.S. government and to opposing rogue nations, LexCorp's own private army tests prototype military tech. The company's Security Sentry brigade is made up of ex-Special Forces, former mercenaries, and other well-trained soldiers of fortune.

LexTek snub-nosed air-cooled automatic pistol with laser sighting and smart-technology safety trigger

INDUSTRIAL ESPIONAGE

LexCorp's scientific patents aren't always internally generated. Luthor's special operatives engage in all manner of industrial espionage, sabotage, and thievery, including stealing research and designs from former LexCorp employee Professor Emil Hamilton!

CRASH

BIZARRO

BY DEFINITION, a "Bizarro" is an imperfect duplicate of Superman. While previous Bizarros were Lex Luthor's failed attempts to clone the Man of Steel, the current creature defies logical explanation. Springing forth from a nightmarish world created when Batman's arch-foe the Joker acquired 99 percent of Mr. Mxyzptlk's Fifth-Dimensional magicks, this Bizarro is everything Superman is not … only worse! Like the distorted image in a funhouse mirror, Bizarro is a twisted reflection of the Man of Tomorrow, with backward superpowers and an upside-down view of right and wrong.

SEND IN THE CLONE

Lex Luthor wanted his own Man of Steel. Secretly scanning Superman's molecular structure, he ordered his top scientist, Dr. Teng, to duplicate his foe. However, neither Luthor nor Teng realized that Superman came from another world. Teng was unable to replicate Kryptonian DNA, resulting in an imperfect clone whose body swiftly mutated into a lumbering "Bizarro" menace!

Despite being held captive by the love-struck Bizarro, Lois mourned the poor creature's demise.

EARLY ADVENTURE

Having only fragmentary genetic memory, the first Bizarro tried to live as a version of Clark Kent before encountering the real Man of Steel. Bizarro #1 gave his life so that the blind Lucy Lane, sister of Lois, might see again. A second Bizarro – another failed clone – built a ramshackle "Bizarro World" to win the affection of his beloved "Lo-iz."

HA-HO! HIM AM BACK!

Wielding Mr. Mxyzptlk's matter-manipulating powers, the Clown Prince of Crime created a cube-shaped Bizarro-Earth with continents hewn in the image of Emperor Joker! Wrong was right on this backward Earth terrorized by a villainous JLA whose roster included the demon Scorch, gun-toting Bounty, armored Ignition, and an all-new Bizarro #1! In a mixed-up Metropolis, Bizarro fought for lies, injustice, and the un-American way, and made his headquarters in the crumbling Graveyard of Solitude!

OPPOSITES REPEL
Though able to match the Man of Steel punch for punch, Bizarro's superpowers are, in other respects, the complete opposite of Superman's. Instead of heat vision, Bizarro's red-irised, yellow-tinged eyes emit freezing beams of ice! And where Superman can compress his breath into concentrated gusts of cold air, Bizarro belches forth gouts of flame!

REAL NAME None
OCCUPATION
Imperfect Duplicate
BASE Mobile
HEIGHT 6 ft 3 in **WEIGHT** 225 lb
EYES Red **HAIR** Black
FIRST APPEARANCE
ACTION COMICS #254
(July 1959)

IMPERFECT LOGIC
With his super-abilities often canceled out by Bizarro's opposing powers, Superman has to rely on other tactics to defeat his chalk-skinned doppelganger. By reverse logic, kryptonite – which is deadly to Superman – only makes the creature stronger. Superman is usually forced into outwitting Bizarro by turning the tables on his imperfect duplicate's upside-down way of thinking.

ZOD'S PAWN
Thanks to Mr. Mxyzptlk, Bizarro survived the Joker's defeat after Earth was restored to normal. He was then captured by Ignition, who turned him over to the evil General Zod. For months, Zod tortured the creature simply to feel the pleasure of hurting a makeshift Man of Steel.

SCRUNCH

81

BRAINIAC

MIND-BENDER

Brainiac's telepathic and psychokinetic powers enable him to bend lesser beings to his will. His consciousness can link with virtually any computer system and pervert its data to his evil ends.

REAL NAME Vril Dox
OCCUPATION Cyber-Conqueror
BASE Mobile
HEIGHT Variable WEIGHT Variable
EYES Red HAIR None
FIRST APPEARANCE
ACTION COMICS #242
(July 1958)

THE MIND OF VRIL DOX is his greatest weapon. Once Scientist Prime of the planet Colu, Dox attempted to overthrow his technologically advanced world's Supreme Authority. Dox paid for this rebellion by being disintegrated. Yet somehow his computer-like mind remained intact, traveling thousands of light-years to Earth. Using his vast telepathic and psychokinetic abilities, Dox possessed the body of a sideshow mentalist named Milton Fine to become the power-hungry villain Brainiac. Time and time again, only Superman has stood in the way of Brainiac's many ingenious schemes to dominate Earth and its people.

Brainiac 2.5 gloats as Superman is disabled by a blast of kryptonite vapor!

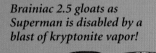

KRYPTONIAN

DOWNLOAD OF EVIL

Milton Fine's body proved too frail to contain Brainiac's powerful consciousness. He sought more suitable hosts, even inhabiting the body of Doomsday and kidnapping the son of Pete and Lana Ross to provide him with genetic material for a new organic body! Failing in those attempts, Brainiac downloaded his evil alien psyche into a flawless android shell, to become Brainiac 2.5.

EARTH'S FINAL HOUR

Brainiac 2.5's plan was simple: unless Superman surrendered himself, the android tyrant's Omega Spears riddling Earth's surface would create an energy web and tear the planet asunder!

BRAINIAC!!!

ALL WIRED UP

As the 20th century gave way to the 21st, Brainiac 2.5 struck, fulfilling fears of worldwide computer crashes. Brainiac turned Earth's nuclear arsenals upon the planet itself. But as annihilation loomed, the android tyrant suffered a programming meltdown!

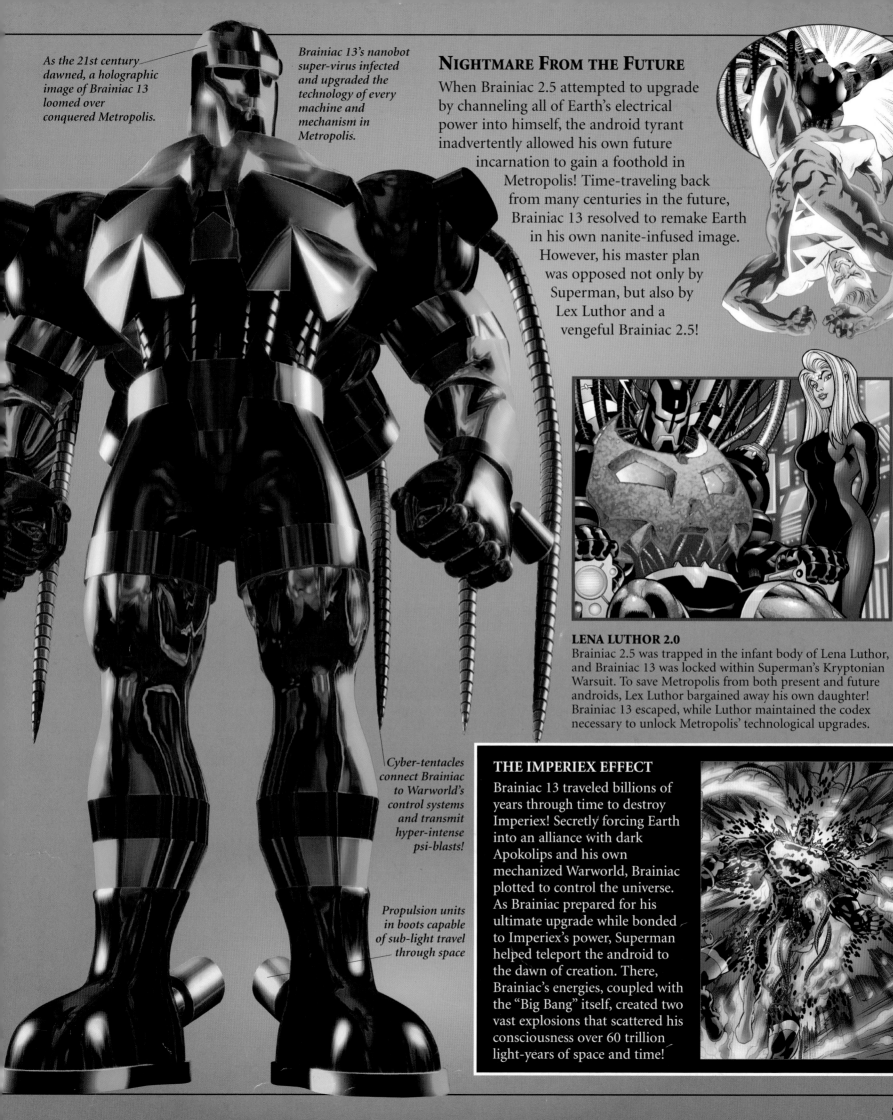

As the 21st century dawned, a holographic image of Brailliac 13 loomed over conquered Metropolis.

Brainiac 13's nanobot super-virus infected and upgraded the technology of every machine and mechanism in Metropolis.

Cyber-tentacles connect Brainiac to Warworld's control systems and transmit hyper-intense psi-blasts!

Propulsion units in boots capable of sub-light travel through space

NIGHTMARE FROM THE FUTURE

When Brainiac 2.5 attempted to upgrade by channeling all of Earth's electrical power into himself, the android tyrant inadvertently allowed his own future incarnation to gain a foothold in Metropolis! Time-traveling back from many centuries in the future, Brainiac 13 resolved to remake Earth in his own nanite-infused image. However, his master plan was opposed not only by Superman, but also by Lex Luthor and a vengeful Brainiac 2.5!

LENA LUTHOR 2.0

Brainiac 2.5 was trapped in the infant body of Lena Luthor, and Brainiac 13 was locked within Superman's Kryptonian Warsuit. To save Metropolis from both present and future androids, Lex Luthor bargained away his own daughter! Brainiac 13 escaped, while Luthor maintained the codex necessary to unlock Metropolis' technological upgrades.

THE IMPERIEX EFFECT

Brainiac 13 traveled billions of years through time to destroy Imperiex! Secretly forcing Earth into an alliance with dark Apokolips and his own mechanized Warworld, Brainiac plotted to control the universe. As Brainiac prepared for his ultimate upgrade while bonded to Imperiex's power, Superman helped teleport the android to the dawn of creation. There, Brainiac's energies, coupled with the "Big Bang" itself, created two vast explosions that scattered his consciousness over 60 trillion light-years of space and time!

DARKSEID

FOR UNTOLD MILLENNIA, the planets New Genesis and Apokolips have warred with one another. While the heroic New Gods of New Genesis believe in peace and harmony, the citizens of dark Apokolips know only oppression and slavery under the crushing heels of Darkseid. Unfortunately, the dreaded Lord of Apokolips will not be satisfied until he rules the entire cosmos! To do so, Darkseid has targeted Earth as the source of the elusive Anti-Life Equation, which will give him dominion over all living creatures, including Superman!

WELCOME TO APOKOLIPS

Dark half of the so-called Fourth World, Apokolips is a dismal orb pocked by giant fire-pits, energy processing plants which belch flames and soot over the planet's surface. The Lowlies, Apokolips' wretched citizens, toil in the dismal Armagetto watched by Paredemons, Darkseid's winged stormtroopers. For many, the only escape from Apokolips is death!

THE DARK LORD

Darkseid has long sought the means to crush New Genesis and rule the cosmos! Once second in succession to the throne of Apokolips, Darkseid murdered his own brother Drax in order to seize the powerful "Omega Effect" and rule his despair-ridden world unopposed. Later, Darkseid's quest for the Anti-Life Equation led him to Metropolis, where he armed Intergang as his advance guard in overrunning Earth. Fortunately, the Man of Steel continues to prevent Darkseid and his minions from gaining a foothold on his adopted world!

REAL NAME
Uxas, Son of Heggra

OCCUPATION Supreme Ruler

BASE Apokolips

HEIGHT 7 ft 6 in **WEIGHT** 515 lb

EYES Red **HAIR** None

FIRST APPEARANCE
SUPERMAN'S PAL
JIMMY OLSEN #134
(October 1971)

THE DOG OF WAR

Darkseid's greatest foe is his own son, Orion! As a boy, he was traded with the heir of New Genesis to secure peace. Orion was raised in the benevolent teachings of Highfather, ruler of New Genesis, yet nurtured a fierce hatred for Darkseid. Feared upon Apokolips as "The Dog of War," Orion now battles to defend New Genesis astride his powerful Astro-Harness.

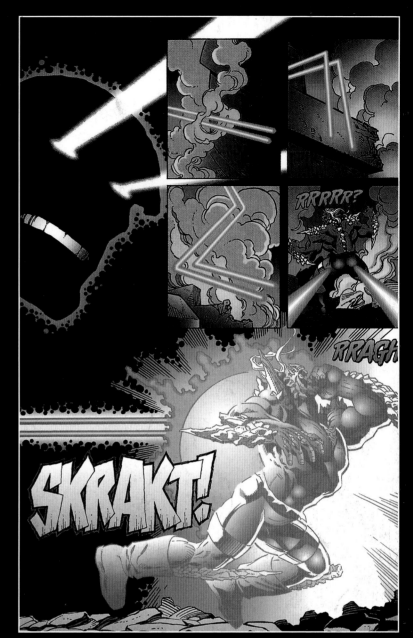

MURDEROUS MINIONS

Darkseid's elite servants are far from trustworthy and would gleefully betray their master if assured success. The robed Desaad is a sadistic schemer who delights in torture. Kalibak the Cruel, a vicious man-beast, is another of Darkseid's raging sons. The nightmarish Granny Goodness delights in bringing pain and suffering to the children of Armagetto imprisoned in her many orphanages.

Desaad's talents lie in the invention of instruments of interrogation and weapons of mass destruction!

In battle, Kalibak wields his Beta-Club, which projects deadly "nerve beams."

Supergirl once found herself at odds with Granny Goodness and her Female Furies, warrior women trained in Darkseid's Special Powers Force.

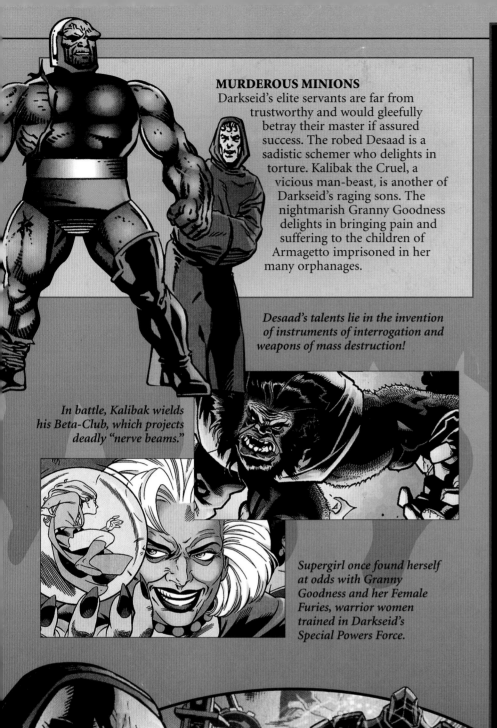

OMEGA BEAMS

When the Doomsday monster was inadvertently transported to Apokolips aboard a cargo ship, Darkseid unleashed his most dreadful weapon: the Omega Effect! From his own eyes Darkseid emits twin energy beams of catastrophic destructive power! The Omega Effect can also transport a foe through time or space, as it did to the unstoppable Doomsday. Or if Darkseid chooses, the beams may be unleashed to resurrect anyone previously destroyed by the Omega Effect.

THE ENTROPY AEGIS

When the all-conquering Imperiex threatened the universe, Darkseid united Apokolips with Earth and its friendly alien allies. One of Darkseid's secret weapons in the war to save creation was the *Entropy Aegis*, an Imperiex-Probe salvaged and retrofitted to become an "anti-venom" weapon against Imperiex. Though refused by Superman, the mortally wounded Steel would later possess this incredibly powerful armor.

ENCANTADORA

LOURDES LUCERO could be Superman's most beguiling foe. With the mystical Mist of Ibella contained in her necklace vial, she is able to cloud men's minds and teleport herself anywhere. Encantadora has engaged in elaborate schemes to support herself and her little brother Victor. One ruse involved selling counterfeit kryptonite to Superman's enemies. Although she has promised to forsake crime, the allure of magic and her attraction to the Man of Steel may be temptations Lourdes cannot resist for long!

MYSTICAL ATTRACTION

Lourdes' father was the first of her family to possess the Mist of Ibella. He resisted its promises of power, but could not bear to throw the vial away. Lourdes watched as the terrible talisman drove her father mad. She vowed to bury the vial beside her dying father, but she also promised to protect and provide for her brother Victor. Ultimately, the Mist won out.

Like an exotic, enticing pheromone, the Mist of Ibella is a powerful force. During a "shopping spree," a trail of spellbound men stumbled over one another to carry 'Dora's ill-gotten gains.

HAAAKGCH!!

THE MOST DANGEROUS GAME

Encantadora never meant the Man of Steel any harm, but the pain he felt convinced him that her kryptonite was all too real. The bewitching beauty intended to sell her glowing green bauble to the highest bidder among a throng of super-villains. Superman eventually saw through 'Dora's deception, realizing that her mysterious power of suggestion was the cause of his weakness, not her fake kryptonite.

REAL NAME
Lourdes Lucero

OCCUPATION Enchantress

BASE Metropolis

HEIGHT 5 ft 7 in **WEIGHT** 135 lb

EYES Brown **HAIR** Brown

FIRST APPEARANCE
ACTION COMICS #760
(December 1999)

Deathstroke conquered Encantadora's charms by disabling her with a concussive disorientation grenade!

FAMILY TIES

Encantadora's biggest mistake was attempting to con "The Demon's Head," Rā's al Ghūl. Batman's arch-foe let her live, but at a price. Hoping to make himself all-powerful, Rā's demanded 'Dora's Mist of Ibella, and held her 10-year-old brother Victor hostage to claim the Mist of Ibella. But with Superman's help, Encantadora recovered the cursed Mist and was happily reunited with Victor.

THE TERMINATOR

As Superman lay dying from kryptonite poisoning, only Encantadora knew why … but Deathstroke the Terminator was determined to make sure her lips remained sealed! Armed with a personal teleportation device to match her transporting Mist, this assassin-for-hire was just one sword-slash away from silencing 'Dora – permanently!

'Dora keeps the crimson Mist of Ibella close to her heart

KISS ME DEADLY

Ironically, Encantadora *did* possess kryptonite when she first met the Man of Steel. While S.T.A.R. Labs physicians raced to save Superman's life, 'Dora revealed that she had been hired to implant a kryptonite-nanobot in the Man of Steel by any means necessary. She did so with a kiss, her poisoned peck resulting in Superman's near-fatal kryptonite tumor. 'Dora's information ultimately saved him from certain death, and Superman would later learn that General Zod, ruler of Pokolistan, was the true culprit behind its poisoning.

DOMINUS

PRIOR TO HIS UNTIMELY disintegration, the being known as Tuoni lived a life of prayer and peaceful meditation. One of five custodians of his world's faith, Tuoni fell in love with his fellow devotee Ahti. But when Ahti ascended past him and assumed the mantle of Kismet, Illuminator of All Realities, jealous Tuoni turned to infernal magicks to replace his former paramour. Dabbling in forbidden sorcery destroyed Tuoni's body, leaving only the vengeance-seeking phantasm known as Dominus!

FOR THE WANT OF KISMET

When the four moons of his world aligned, Tuoni watched in horror as his lover Ahti was granted the divine powers he coveted and became Kismet. Paying no heed to the dangers, Tuoni consulted ancient magical texts to usurp Kismet's mantle. Despite Tuoni's betrayal, Kismet showed mercy, shunting his body into the Kryptonian limbo known as the Phantom Zone!

Tuoni and Ahti before jealousy tore them apart.

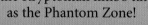

Godlike in power, Kismet illuminates the myriad divergent pathways of reality. She can warp and bend the very fabric of the universe to her bidding.

As Tuoni tried to seize Kismet's power, his energies were deflected back at him, vaporizing his body!

THE KRYPTONIAN CONNECTION

The Man of Steel's connection to the reality-altering rogue was closer than he ever imagined. When Kismet placed the still-living remains of Tuoni in the Phantom Zone, a holographic projection of Superman's ancestor Kem-L – discoverer of the inter-dimensional void –used Kryptonian technology to reconstruct Tuoni's body. Reborn as Dominus, Tuoni escaped the Zone via Superman's Fortress of Solitude and laid waste to his native planet.

MIND CONTROL

Thanks to Kem-L's Kryptonian technology and the arcane knowledge he gleaned before his physical body was destroyed, Dominus easily manipulates the minds of lesser beings. His greatest power is the ability to mine the subconscious fears of his victims to create divergent realities based on their worst nightmares.

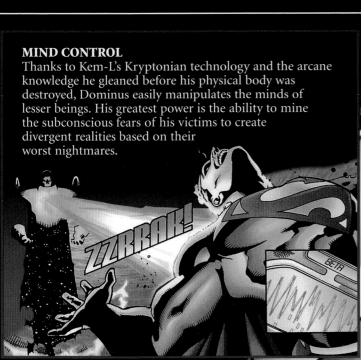

REAL NAME Unknown
OCCUPATION Destroyer of Worlds
BASE The Infinite Domain
HEIGHT Unknown WEIGHT Unknown
EYES Red HAIR None
FIRST APPEARANCE
ACTION COMICS # 747
(August 1998)

CAPTIVE DOMINUS

Following his escape from the Phantom Zone, Dominus tried to find Kismet and claim her power. Thanks to the Man of Steel, he failed. In revenge, Dominus sifted through Superman's insecurities and convinced him that Earth would descend into chaos unless Superman ruled it himself. The Man of Steel then created an army of Superman Robots to police every corner of the globe!

INTO THE ABYSS

Dominus nearly turned Earth against the Man of Steel. He succeeded in destroying Superman's Fortress. But he could not break Kal-El's spirit. Using the Kryptonian warrior discipline known as *Torquasm-Vo*, Superman defeated Dominus and returned him to the Phantom Zone. There, the billion souls of his victims dragged him down into the dark void.

BLOAT AND SHREWFACE

Two of the stranger characters associated with Intergang, simple-minded burglars Mortimer Slake (a.k.a. "Shrew-Face") and Hannibal Leach (a.k.a. "Mr. Bloat") are classified by the Metropolis S.C.U. as "Magnitude-10 Meta-Criminals." Shrew-Face's dangerous matter-phasing powers allow him to rearrange the atomic structure of organic substances. The aptly named Mr. Bloat is a matter-osmosifier who absorbs any material he touches into his own blubbery body.

Easily distressed, the skittish Tsarina leads the Russian Mafia in Metropolis.

STRYKER'S ISLAND

Metropolis's Maximum Security Correctional Facility boasts that it is the "ultimate prison" following the 200-year-old penitentiary's millennial upgrade by Brainiac 13. In addition to its population of criminal "normals," Stryker's Island also incarcerates a host of dangerous metahuman villains in its 2,456 cell units and 108 solitary confinement cubicles. Many of the meta-villain shackling systems and high-tech escape deterrents are provided by both John Henry Irons and S.T.A.R. Labs.

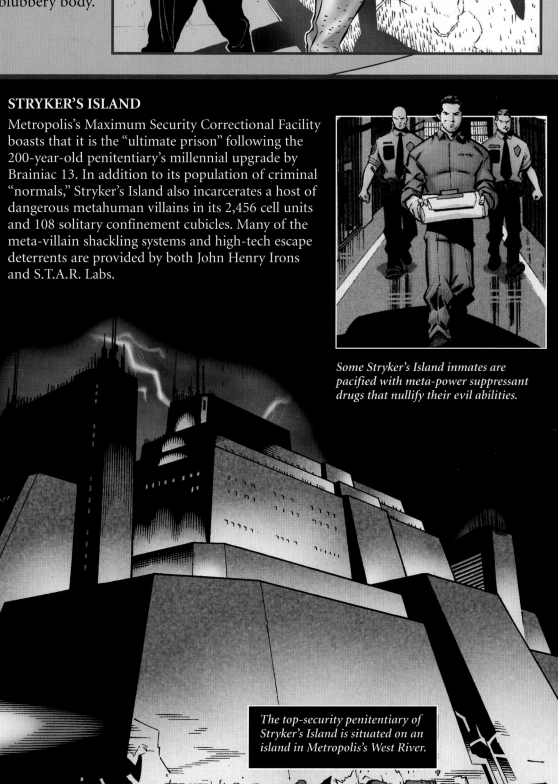

Some Stryker's Island inmates are pacified with meta-power suppressant drugs that nullify their evil abilities.

The top-security penitentiary of Stryker's Island is situated on an island in Metropolis's West River.

TSARINA

The Ukrainian-born "Tsarina" (real name unrevealed) is hoping to make a royal name for herself in the Metropolis underworld. Her gang of Ukrainian émigrés brought to life a set of giant *Matryoshka*, Russian nesting dolls that vandalized the *Daily Planet* globe before Superman took matters in hand.

HUMAN HORRORS

MADNESS, MENTAL ILLNESS, AND MEGALOMANIA are common denominators linking six of Superman's most erratic enemies. One is merely misguided, a hero in his own injured mind. Two are deranged by revenge fantasies fulfilled by terrible toys and pernicious pranks. Another's chronic insomnia is made worse by the incessant laughter of his devilish duplicates. An imaginary fifth foe should never have been, but was willed into life by a troubled boy in need of help. And the remaining raving rogue seeks nothing less than to forever erase Superman's own existence across time and space!

Powered up, the Atomic Skull is a walking nuclear reactor!

GOG

In a possible future, a man known as William will come to believe that Superman is responsible for the nuclear devastation of Kansas and the annihilation of millions. Armed with that knowledge and an energy-blasting battle-staff, William – who once sang Superman's praises – will rename himself "Gog" and travel throughout Hypertime to kill the Supermen of alternate realities in order to prevent the Midwestern Apocalypse. Pray he doesn't succeed.

ATOMIC SKULL

Exposure to an alien "gene-bomb" gave Joe Martin heightened strength and the ability to emit blasts of radioactive energy. It also rendered his flesh invisible. While seeking medical treatment, Martin suffered head injuries that left him delusional. He now believes himself to be the "Atomic Skull," a hero from his favorite 1930s movie serials.

Martin lapses into his "Atomic Skull" persona despite ongoing psychological treatment. Aboard his flying Skull-Bike, he seeks out Lois Lane, a dead-ringer for the late Eleanor Hart, an actress who once played the Atomic Skull's love-interest, Zelda Wentworth!

RIOT

Scientist Frederick Legion used a temporal phase shifter to "borrow" copies of himself from microseconds in the future in order to complete several experiments at once. Ultimately, Frederick's duplications left him severely sleep-deprived, disfiguring his mind and body in the process. Now able to replicate at will, Frederick embarked on a life of crime as the madcap Riot.

ADVERSARY

By his own estimation, the Adversary was "the toughest $#*%¢ on the planet!" But he never really existed in the first place. Braniac 13's citywide upgrade of Metropolis's machinery also affected beings of higher consciousness, causing the psychic talents of a crippled boy named Cary Richards to suddenly manifest. The Adversary was Cary's imagination made real, a worthy foe to challenge his hero Superman. Once a pawn of the demonic Satanus, Cary was freed from imprisonment in the netherworld by Superman, who hasn't tussled with the Adversary since.

TOYMAN

In happier times, Winslow Schott was a simple toymaker lauded for his inventive playthings. But LexCorp's acquisition of Schott's toy company left him jobless and burning for revenge against Lex Luthor. Schott's failed attempts to kill Luthor with weaponized toys eventually led to an association with Intergang and a subsequent criminal career.

PRANKSTER

Oswald Loomis owes his trim, dapper appearance to Satanus. He was once the buck-toothed and portly host of WGBS TV's "The Uncle Oswald Show." After his early morning children's program was canceled due to low ratings, Loomis tried unsuccessfully to kill WGBS owner Morgan Edge with an arsenal of deadly comedic pranks. When Superman intervened, Loomis decided to remain in the spotlight by becoming the Prankster.

Loomis continues to improve his bag of deadly dime-store tricks.

DEMONS OF DOOM

WOOLK...!

IF GOOD AND EVIL are opposing forces locked in eternal conflict, it should come as no surprise that the virtuous Man of Steel finds himself continually beset by spirits embodying the powers of darkness. Superman's vulnerability to magic turns his encounters with the devilish Satanus or his sinister sibling Blaze into battles for his own incorruptible spirit! And even when the Silver Banshee, Mudge, or Scorch are unable to taint Kal-El's indomitable will, these lesser demons know they can wound the Last Son of Krypton by striking at his loved ones!

MUDGE

Little is known of the demon Mudge, except that he aided his master, Lord Satanus, in an attempt to possess post-Y2K Metropolis. Satanus' slimy, serpentine-tongued underling battled Thorn and helped to abduct Cary Richards, a young boy whose psionic powers nearly led to the demonic domination of the city!

SATANUS

Evil incarnate, Lord Satanus desires one thing: Superman's soul! Satanus rules over an infernal netherworld, the seat of his dreadful supernatural might and the staging ground for his assaults upon the Man of Steel. Though he sometimes wields a hellfire-blasting gnarled staff, his very body is a conduit of powerful, eldritch energies. The dark lord's mortal guise is the dashing Collin Thornton, the Metropolis-based publisher of *Newstime* magazine, former employer of Clark Kent!

BLAZE

The demoness Blaze steals the psychic life essences of humans unfortunate enough to fall under her terrible thrall. She rules her own fiery realm, while vying for control of her brother Satanus's domain.

THE SILVER BANSHEE
The siren wail of the Silver Banshee is a deadly song. Once denied leadership of her Irish clan, Siobhan McDougal's attempts at mystical intervention resulted in her banishment to the netherverse. Siobhan eventually found revenge when the mysterious Crone empowered her to return to Earth as the Silver Banshee! Superman thwarted Siobhan's first vengeful attack. However, a remorseful Silver Banshee later spared the life of Lacy MacElwain, sole survivor of the clan McDougal, forever uniting the two women in their tragic family curse.

Impervious to gunfire, possessing the strength of ten men and superhuman speed, the Silver Banshee is a formidable foe. Her witchy wail is death to any victim in sight of the skull-faced succubus.

SCORCH

With her flaming touch, Scorch heated up the Joker's League of Anarchy. She was a devilish doppelganger of the angelic Supergirl, right down to her close-cropped raven hair and pointed prehensile tail. Though the Clown Prince of Crime was defeated and reality righted, Scorch somehow survived, just like several other JLA menaces whom Mr. Mxyzptlk helped to jump over to the "real" world.

ALIEN ALERT

HIS EVIL ENEMIES are not limited to Earth-bound menaces and malefactors. In fact, Superman's Rogues Gallery includes invaders from the stars and beyond! The alluring Maxima wanted the Man of Steel to be her mate. Ignition is an enigma that first appeared on a mad world only the Joker could envision. Massacre is a marauding hunter seeking worthy prey. General Zod and Faora bear the same names as Kryptonian foes thought long dead. And Kancer is a monster bred inside Kal-El's own body!

IGNITION
A product of the Joker's twisted mind, Ignition first appeared on the "Bizarro-Earth" created by the Mxyzptlk-empowered Clown Prince of Crime. Thought to have dissolved after the Joker's defeat, Ignition was given new life by Mr. Mxyzptlk. The armored dynamo now serves as an engine of evil loyal to General Zod.

MAXIMA
The alien empress Maxima desired a mate worthy of ruling the planet Almerac alongside her. When the Last Son of Krypton refused to become her consort, Maxima used her psychokinetic powers in several vain attempts to convince him otherwise. Ironically, she died in defense of Earth in the struggle against Imperiex.

After Almerac was destroyed by Imperiex, Maxima sided with Earth in the resulting intergalactic war.

MASSACRE
Since their first encounter, the alien killer Massacre has been obsessed with making Superman another of his victims. Able to read opponents' nerve impulses and predict their moves, the super-tough Massacre travels the galaxy spoiling for his next great battle. He can convert his body into energy, moving from planet to planet at light-speed in search of bloodsport.

Last of the royal line of Almerac, Maxima possessed heightened mental and physical powers, including the ability to molecularly manipulate matter.

KANCER

Malignant and murderous, Kancer began its life as a tumor inside Superman's kryptonite-poisoned body. Stolen from S.T.A.R. Labs after its removal, the alien carcinoma was mutated into a monster by the evil General Zod. Kancer's toxic touch breaks down living cellular structures.

FAORA

Superman has met three other women called "Faora." One belonged to a trio of Kryptonians who decimated a parallel universe Earth. The second was a Kryptonian terrorist. The third Faora uses her power to disrupt molecular bonds while serving as second-in-command to General Zod.

GENERAL ZOD

Like Faora, the appellation "Zod" is familiar to the Man of Steel. The first Zod is long dead, having destroyed all life on a parallel Earth. Superman can only assume that the dictatorial General Zod he once met on Krypton suffered the same fate as that doomed planet. Now a new General Zod has emerged. The ruler of the war-torn European republic of Pokolistan, Zod poses a grave threat to world peace and to Superman's health!

NEW ENEMIES

IN HIS NEVER-ENDING BATTLE against the forces of evil and injustice, the Man of Steel realizes full well that the ranks of his rogues gallery will be replenished with new and even more dangerous foes. Power corrupts. And the powers wielded by supervillains corrupt them absolutely. Some of the following new foes are macabre minions of Superman's arch-foe Lex Luthor. Others are misguided heroes from another dimension entirely, forced through circumstance into battling Superman and his allies.

REPLIKON
An alien adversary who had not been seen by the Man of Steel for nearly six years, Replikon's extraterrestrial technology allowed him to replicate the powers of the entire Justice League, making him a truly formidable foe. When Replikon returned, he was in thrall to Ruin and forced to fight Superman, a battle that cost the villain his life!

MASTER JAILER
Carl Draper, the Master Jailer, was recruited by Manchester Black to carry out a revenge scheme upon the Man of Steel. The Master Jailer prided himself on his ability to create chains to manacle any superpowered being, including Superman.

THE LEGION OF SUPER-VILLAINS
They came from the future, (left to right) Saturn Queen, Lightning Lord, and Cosmic King, a trio of time-traveling super-villains who abducted baby Kal-El before he could be found by the Kents, as well as plucking Bruce Wayne from the moment in time after his parents were murdered. Raising both boys as their own children, this Legion of Super-Villains created an alternate timeline in which Superman and Batman ruled Earth without pity. Fortunately, some heroes remained to right the timeline and defeat the evil Legion.

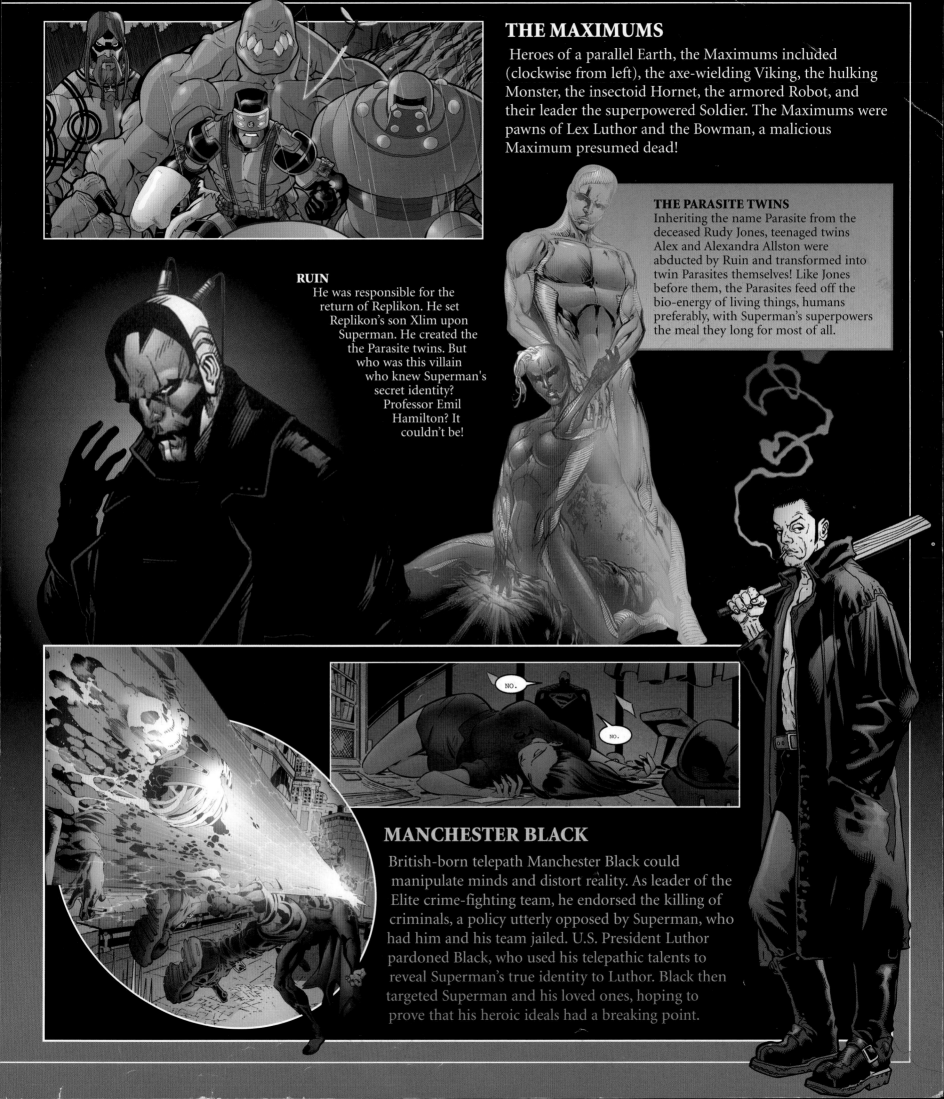

THE MAXIMUMS

Heroes of a parallel Earth, the Maximums included (clockwise from left), the axe-wielding Viking, the hulking Monster, the insectoid Hornet, the armored Robot, and their leader the superpowered Soldier. The Maximums were pawns of Lex Luthor and the Bowman, a malicious Maximum presumed dead!

THE PARASITE TWINS

Inheriting the name Parasite from the deceased Rudy Jones, teenaged twins Alex and Alexandra Allston were abducted by Ruin and transformed into twin Parasites themselves! Like Jones before them, the Parasites feed off the bio-energy of living things, humans preferably, with Superman's superpowers the meal they long for most of all.

RUIN

He was responsible for the return of Replikon. He set Replikon's son Xlim upon Superman. He created the the Parasite twins. But who was this villain who knew Superman's secret identity? Professor Emil Hamilton? It couldn't be!

MANCHESTER BLACK

British-born telepath Manchester Black could manipulate minds and distort reality. As leader of the Elite crime-fighting team, he endorsed the killing of criminals, a policy utterly opposed by Superman, who had him and his team jailed. U.S. President Luthor pardoned Black, who used his telepathic talents to reveal Superman's true identity to Luthor. Black then targeted Superman and his loved ones, hoping to prove that his heroic ideals had a breaking point.

SUPERMAN'S CAREER

DC COMICS' SUPERMAN may not be pulp fiction's first costumed hero, but he is undeniably the most enduring. Writer Jerry Siegel and artist Joe Shuster didn't merely envision a tin god battling injustice in the debut issue of *Action Comics*, they brought to life a Man of Steel, an interstellar orphan from a dying world blasted to Earth in a tiny rocket to be raised by simple God-fearing folk. The clear allusions to the biblical story of Moses were not lost on Siegel or Shuster. They decided that, like the good son of Pharaoh, Superman would emerge from these humble beginnings to lead his people, from the townsfolk of Smallville to the millions of Metropolis and beyond, to a better world. With the timeless character of Superman, Siegel and Shuster didn't just create the world's most beloved comic book hero. They created the *ideal* hero, whose unflagging virtue and undefeatable optimism inspire every single one of us to want to be just like him. The cape is optional!